HORACE

Horace *Odes* II

Vatis Amici

DAVID WEST

CLARENDON PRESS · OXFORD
1998

Oxford University Press, Great Clarendon Street, Oxford OX2 6DP
Oxford New York
Athens Auckland Bangkok Bogotá Buenos Aires Calcutta
Cape Town Chennai Dar es Salaam Delhi Florence Hong Kong Istanbul
Karachi Kuala Lumpur Madrid Melbourne Mexico City Mumbai
Nairobi Paris São Paolo Singapore Taipei Tokyo Toronto Warsaw
and associated companies in
Berlin Ibadan

Oxford is a registered trade mark of Oxford University Press

Published in the United States
by Oxford University Press Inc., New York

First published 1998

British Library Cataloguing in Publication Data
Data available

Library of Congress Cataloging in Publication Data
Data available
ISBN 0–19–872162–5
ISBN 0–19–872163–3 (Pbk)

1 3 5 7 9 10 8 6 4 2

Typeset by Hope Services (Abingdon) Ltd.
Printed in Great Britain on acid-free paper by
Biddles Ltd., Guildford & King's Lynn

Preface

Horace is one of the world's greatest lyric poets, but not one of the most accessible. I would like this book to do three things: to help non-Latinists who like poetry to enjoy Horace; to stimulate young people who have to study the poems; and to add to the scholarly debate by putting forward my own views, which seem on occasion to go against present-day orthodoxies. Horace is a profound poet of love, religion, and friendship, with a rich sense of humour and love of fantasy, a master of tone and pace and shape. The book tries to demonstrate this by translating the poems in versions slightly adjusted from those printed in the volume in the World's Classics series, *The Complete Odes and Epodes of Horace* (Oxford, 1997), and by providing brief comments to describe how the poetry works. A knowledge of Latin is not necessary. Since the first few odes happen to require rather elaborate commentaries, readers new to Horace are advised to start with poems 4–8.

The title of this book is the last two words of *Odes* 2.6, where Horace calls himself friend and bard, the word translated as bard being *vates*, which means that Horace sees himself as poet, priest, and prophet of the Augustan regime. As *amicus* he addresses thirteen contemporary figures in these twenty odes. Five of the poems, 12, 13, 17, 18, 20, concern Maecenas, one of the chief ministers of Augustus, who was also Horace's patron and, if the poems are to be believed, his dearest friend. The book is, amongst other things, an Art of Friendship.

Realizing that *Carpe Diem*, my commentary on the first book of the Odes (1995*a*), is light on theory, I have tried to explain my views on some such questions as they arose in the course of Book 2: on intertextuality, puns, and metapoetic interpretations, for example, at the end of my notes on *Odes* 6, 8, and 9. These views are usually negative. The reason is that for me literary theory is worse than a waste of words. If we approach poems with a theory in mind, we shall see what we expect to see. My own theory is that the duty of those who write about literature is to point out what is there and, where necessary, explain it historically. The target is to understand the texts as they were understood by contemporary readers. This is impossible since no two contemporary readers reacted identically, and no one reader reacted in the afternoon as he had reacted in the morning. You cannot step into the same book twice. Besides, we belong to our own time and cannot read as though we belonged to another. Nevertheless, the target is worth aiming at. Over the years we have come closer to a historical understanding of Latin literature and of the people who made it and read it.

The advantage is that this experience of different lives enriches our own, and our experience of people of Horace's calibre enriches us hugely. The profit in reading literature is not in its relevance, but in its irrelevance. An atheist lives more if he listens to Bach and reads George Herbert.

Those who wish to go further with Horace are advised to use the commentaries on Books 1 and 2 of the *Odes* by Nisbet and Hubbard (Oxford, 1970 and 1978). I never study an ode of Horace without finding help and inspiration in their work.

D.W.

Contents

Introduction

THE LIFE OF HORACE

Quintus Horatius Flaccus was born in 65 BC in Venusia, a town in central southern Italy near where the regions Lucania and Apulia met. His father was an auctioneer's agent, owned a small farm, and was a freedman, that is a slave who had been freed in his lifetime. He took a great interest in his son's education, taking him to Rome to study Greek, and sending him to Athens, where his principal study was Greek philosophy. On the Ides of March 44 BC Julius Caesar was assassinated by conspirators led by Brutus and Cassius. Brutus then withdrew to Athens, and while attending lectures in philosophy and gathering an army, he recruited young Horace with the rank of *tribunus militum*, the second level of legionary command under the *legatus*. After the conspirators were defeated in 42 BC by Antony and Octavian* at the battle of Philippi, Horace returned to Rome and purchased an administrative post as assistant to the magistrates, a treasury official, *scriba quaestorius*. In 38 BC he was introduced to Maecenas, friend and adviser of Octavian. Horace's first book of *Satires* appeared in 35 BC, and soon after that, thanks to the generosity of Maecenas, he became the happy owner of an estate in the Sabine country. In 31 BC Octavian defeated Antony and Cleopatra at the battle of Actium and in 27 BC he took the title of Augustus. The *Epodes* and a second book of *Satires* appeared in 30 BC, the first three books of *Odes* in 23, the *Epistles* in 19, the *Secular Hymn* in 17, the fourth book of *Odes* in 13 BC and at about the same time the second book of *Epistles*. Maecenas died in 8 BC and in his will, by which he left all his property to Augustus, there is a clause: 'Be mindful of Horatius Flaccus as though he were myself', *Horati Flacci ut mei memor esto*. Horace died fifty-nine days later and the two men were buried close to one another on Maecenas' estate on the Esquiline Hill in Rome.

* Augustus was born Gaius Octavius in 63 BC. In 44 BC he was adopted as son by his great-uncle Julius Caesar under the name of Gaius Iulius Caesar Octavianus (normally called Octavian in English).

These are bare facts. It is not easy to relate them to the poetic personality which Horace fashioned from these materials. Pride in his birthplace is an important element in his poetry, as attested in his *Satires* 2. 1. 34–41:

> I do not know whether I am a Lucanian or an Apulian,
> since the Venusian farmer ploughs on the border between the two,
> sent there, according to tradition, when the Samnites were driven out,
> to make sure that Rome's enemies could not attack over open ground
> whether it was the Apulians or fierce Lucanians who threatened war.
> But this pen of mine will attack no living creature unless provoked.
> It will guard me while it stays hidden in its sheath.

Horace refers to his descent from this sturdy Italian stock in many places in his lyric poetry, sometimes, as here, to insist upon his own loyalty and his own independence, sometimes to delight in the Italian landscape as in the bird's eye view of his native mountains at 3. 4. 14–16, sometimes to praise the peoples of Italy as at 3. 6. 37–44 and 3. 23, and often to reflect upon his achievement in coming from such a background to give the Latin language a body of poetry which can stand beside the great lyric poetry of Greece (3. 13 and 30). It is relevant also to remember that Octavian cultivated the peoples of Italy and they were solidly in his favour. As early as 36 BC the Italian cities were putting up statues of him in their temples (Cassius Dio, 49. 15).

Horace's father poses a puzzle which has only recently been solved by Williams (1995). How could a freedman of modest means have afforded to take his son to school in Rome and send him to mix with the sons of the great at university in Athens? How could a freedman's son in his early twenties so impress Brutus that he was recruited to a rank which meant that he might be called upon to command a Roman legion? And how could he come back to Rome after the defeat at Philippi and purchase an important and lucrative post in political administration?

First of all, these facts have to be read in the contexts in which Horace presents them, as in *Satires* 1. 6. 45–52:

> Now I come back to my own case, the freedman's son
> whom everybody sneers at because I'm a freedman's son.
> They do it now because I live with you. They did it before
> because I was a tribune and had a legion under my command.
> The two cases are different. People might be right
> to envy my rank, but not your friendship, above all
> because you recruit only those who are worthy of it
> and have nothing to do with social climbers.

The poem is clearly a testament of gratitude and admiration from Horace to his father. But it is also a tribute to Horace's patron Maecenas, and its thrust is to establish the character of Maecenas by arguing that he judges men according to their merits. To increase the merits of Maecenas, Horace diminishes his own. His father's freedman status is a gibe (see p. xxii below) which Horace has had to endure and which he is now turning to advantage. Further, his father's occupation as an auctioneer's agent, *coactor*, was not such a humble position as it may sound in English. The *coactor*'s role was to collect the purchase money from the bidder and transmit it to the seller. He would not have failed to take his percentage. In these troubled times where rich properties were being confiscated and booty was coming on the market, great fortunes were made by agents as well as auctioneers. But the essence of the argument rests upon a reconstruction of the history of Venusia. Venusia was the only Latin colony to join the enemies of Rome in the Social War of 91–88 BC. It was stormed by the Romans in 88 BC and more than 3,000 prisoners were taken. *If*—and Williams admits that this is only a hypothesis—Horace's grandfather and father were among those captured, there are parallels which suggest that they might have been sold as slaves. After the Social War Roman citizenship was granted to the peoples of Italy, but before this could be taken up, those who had been captured and enslaved would have had to be manumitted. To call such men freedmen would be a good schoolboy's gibe, but it would be 'a gross travesty of the facts' (Williams 1995: 309). And it would not explain how Horace's father was able to give his son an education that would bring him into contact with the greatest men of Rome. The answer to the puzzle is that Horace, in spite of his own evidence, was wealthy and well connected. He was also shrewd and agreeable. And perhaps Brutus saw that he had inherited some financial acumen from his father, which would make him useful in military administration. This same talent was no doubt relevant also to his future appointment as a treasury official.

THE ODES OF BOOK 2

The first three books of Horace's odes were published in 23 BC. They are short poems written in metres used by the Greek lyric poets, particularly Alcaeus and Sappho, and they touch upon a wide variety of topics including politics, love, friendship, ageing, death, and enjoyment of life (below called *Carpe Diem* poems), ethics, and poetry. The character of the second book will emerge from a quick survey which arranges the poems according to the above categories, despite the fact that no poem deals only with the topic under which it is discussed.

Politics

Odes 2. 1, *Motum ex Metello consule civicum*, praises the great Gaius Asinius Pollio, who had refused to join Octavian in his campaign against Antony and Cleopatra. His literary masterpiece was a history of the Civil Wars, and Horace's poem celebrates that lost work by giving an account of the Wars which seems at many points to recall the very words of Pollio.

Odes 2. 2, *Nullus argento color est*, taking the form of a meditation on the proper use of wealth, praises Crispus Sallustius and Gaius Proculeius, both of whom were agents of Augustus, Sallustius succeeding Maecenas as his most trusted minister (alongside Agrippa), and Proculeius being Maecenas' brother-in-law.

Odes 2. 3, *Aequam memento rebus in arduis servare mentem*, advises Dellius to enjoy his life in view of the certainty of death. Dellius, the 'stunt-rider of the Civil Wars', *desultor bellorum civilium*, was notorious for his nimbleness in changing sides during the 30s BC, typically switching from Antony to Octavian just before Octavian's victory at Actium. A pattern is emerging. Horace was, amongst other things, a praise poet, and his patron was Maecenas. Hence *Odes* 2. 2, which praises men who served Augustus, one of whom was related to Maecenas. Hence *Odes* 2. 1, which praises a great Roman who had not supported Octavian at Actium. Octavian had won the world by his victory at Actium, and had no intention of losing it. He planned to survive, and part of that plan was a programme of forgiveness and reconciliation, of *clementia* and *concordia*. Hence too *Odes* 2. 3, which addresses a man whose loyalty had veered throughout the crucial years, but who has been welcomed into the harmony and stability of the new order. A similar strategy is detectable in six of the first seven poems of Book 1. Horace is an Augustan poet and this is part of his contribution to the Augustan settlement.

Confirmation of this interpretation may be found in *Odes* 2. 7, *O saepe mecum tempus in ultimum deducte*, in which Horace welcomes back to Rome his friend Pompeius who had fought at his side for Brutus and Cassius against Octavian and Antony at Philippi in 42 BC. Since then Horace had been accepted by the new regime, but Pompeius had fought on until the amnesty offered by Octavian in 30 BC. This poem demonstrates the tact and sophistication of which Horace was capable. He praises Augustus in the first stanza without mentioning him, but he also shows total warmth of affection for the friend who had fought alongside him and who had kept up the fight for a dozen years against the man who now ruled the world. The complexity of Horace's response includes the cheerful recall of the mad days the two had known together on campaign, a sidelong glance at the naïvety of their youth and their empty blustering before the battle, and the incompetence and hollow virtue of Brutus, their general. Pompeius would have been pleased with this—he could not have imagined a warmer welcome—and Augustus would have approved. It had again demonstrated that *clementia* which was a key element in his public policy.

Odes 2. 10, *Rectius vives, Licini*, reads like one and the same thing said nine times, nine statements of the importance of the Golden Mean, but closer scrutiny reveals subtle variations, developments, and cross-references which give the poem a vigorous poetic logic. One of the most valuable features of the great commentary by Nisbet and Hubbard is their determined attempt to throw light on every poem by bringing into their discussion anything relevant which is known about the addressees. The addressee in this poem is Licinius Murena, brother-in-law of Maecenas, famed for his rough tongue and untamed temper, who was to be found guilty of conspiracy against Augustus the year after these odes were published. Taking this historical background into consideration, we see that Horace is letting it be known where he stands, warning Licinius of his danger, and justifying Augustus publicly in advance for whatever action he may deem necessary against Licinius. Licinius was executed.

Odes 2. 15, *Iam pauca aratro iugera*, sounds like a stern philosopher protesting against the building of villas and the spread of luxurious estates where once there had been agriculture, but close reading shows that it is also a poem in praise of Augustus. Praise poetry was a refined art-form in the Augustan court, and the essence of praise was that it should be subtle and oblique and should be uttered as though by a man free to be truthful (West 1994*a*: 61). The Greek poet and Epicurean philosopher Philodemus was the adviser of Calpurnius Piso, consul 58 BC, and was responsible for designing and stocking the great library in his Villa dei Papiri at Herculaneum. A recently deciphered fragment of his dialogue 'On Flattery' reveals that the young Virgil and Quintilius Varus were interlocutors in that dialogue, in which Philodemus is at great pains to distinguish between the flatterer and the friend (see Gigante, Auricchio, and West 1996*a*: 6–7). Horace was a friend of Virgil's and the poems of both of them are evidence for their interest in that distinction and the finesse and integrity with which they upheld it.

Love

Odes 2. 4 and 2. 5 plunge into love, but Horace does not beat his breast. Even here he is an Augustan. Augustus intended to make Rome the greatest and the most beautiful of cities, and to create in that city a cultural renaissance and a moral and religious revival. A cultural renaissance requires a literature, and as compared with the achievements of Athens, old Rome was a backwater, with no Latin writing to rival the Greek except the great didactic poem of Lucretius, 'On the Nature of Things', *De Rerum Natura*. Pastoral poetry came to Rome with Virgil's *Eclogues* in 39 BC and satire with Horace's first book in 35 BC. Didactic was served again by Virgil's *Georgics* in 30, and throughout the 20s he was known to be working on the *Aeneid*, a Roman epic to set beside Homer's *Iliad* and *Odyssey*. But against the miracles of the Greek lyric poets, to mention only Sappho, Alcaeus, and Pindar, all Rome could show was two poems in the Sapphic metre by Catullus, one of them a translation. Enter Horace to fill that gap in the Augustan renaissance, the bringer of Greek lyric poetry to Rome. But love was an essential ingredient in Greek lyric poetry, and Horace, knowing that it is difficult to talk about love, found a role for himself as an instructor in the art, a *Praeceptor Amoris*, a middle-aged man of the world observing the extravagances of the young, mocking gently and giving counsel. Hence his advice in *Odes* 2. 4, *Ne sit ancillae tibi amor pudori*, to Xanthias of Phocis not to be ashamed of his love for a slave girl with lovely arms and face and shapely calves. Horace, of course, is past all that. He is over 40.

In *Odes* 2. 5, *Nondum subacta ferre iugum valet cervice*, he acts the same part, advising an unnamed friend not to be in a hurry. If he is patient and allows the girl he desires to grow up, in due course he will love her more than any girl or boy he has loved before. Horace names three of them in glowing terms.

These two poems demonstrate characteristic Horatian changes of tone. *Odes* 2. 4, *Ne sit ancillae*, starts by comparing Xanthias' amorous embarrassment to the experiences of three of the great heroes of Homer's *Iliad*, and moves to ironies directed not only against Xanthias but also against Horace himself. *Odes* 2. 5 begins with a vivid sustained metaphor, moves to another in the third stanza, and returns to the original image in the fourth, before a luxurious passage evoking 'the artificial, amoral world of Hellenistic poetry' (Nisbet and Hubbard 1978: 79).

Odes 2. 8, *Vlla si iuris tibi peierati poena*, is another love poem, and another in which Horace speaks as an amused observer of the experiences of others. It is addressed to a woman whose beauty remains flawless over the years, who lies to all her lovers, and never loses one of them. For some this is the most amusing poem he ever wrote; for others it is spoilt by an allusion to the importance of smell in sexual attraction. In bringing Greek love lyric to Italy as part of the Augustan renaissance, Horace is not going to stop short. There are indelicacies in Greek lyric poets, and Horace has a taste for danger.

Friendship

Odes 2. 7, a testament of friendship, has already been discussed in terms of its political implications. In *Odes* 2. 6, *Septimi, Gadis aditure mecum*, affection for Septimius glows on the page but we see also Horace's love of Greece and of Italy. He loves Greek poetry and is steeped in it, but he also loves things Italian, particularly the places, the people, and the produce. This too is Augustan. Augustus put himself forward as the leader of Italy, and as a defender of the heritage of the towns and countryside of Italy after they had suffered the ravages of civil war for a century. The praise of Italy which occurs in Virgil, *Georgics* 2. 136–76 and in *Odes* 2. 6 is in accord with the interests of Augustus that Italy should be praised and compared favourably with Greece. This poem, too, has a political dimension.

Friendship brings us to Maecenas. *Odes* 2. 17, *Cur me querelis exanimas tuis*, is a message of cheer to Horace's friend, who has been ill and is not convinced that he is cured. Horace speaks with intense affection and gratitude, and even here, in the contemplation of death, with touches of humour. The end of the poem shows that in the subtle conversations of this intimate friendship Horace does not forget that Maecenas is the patron and Horace the beneficiary. Patronage and friendship can subsist together and great art is sometimes financially rewarded.

Odes 2. 12, *Nolis longa ferae bella Numantiae*, is a poem in an established form—the *recusatio*, in which the poet praises while declining to praise. The normal features of the form are well known, and the variations played by the poet show that he can write within an established tradition with freedom and imagination. This writing is at once derivative and innovative, and Horace uses the tradition to praise Augustus, to create powerful historical and mythological analogies, to tease his friend Maecenas, and, if the interpretation offered on pages 83–6 is correct, to compliment Maecenas' wife and refer to his notorious affection for her. The form is common, but the poem is Horatian.

Carpe Diem
Odes 2. 11, *Quid bellicosus Cantaber et Scythes*, advises Quinctius to enjoy his life in view of the certainty of death. The paraphrase suits this poem as well as it suits *Odes* 2. 3, which has already been looked at as a political poem. This does not prove the paucity of Horace's thought, but its complexity and the treachery of paraphrase. Differences could be listed—2. 11 glances at Epicurean ethical thinking in line 5, at what we lose as we age, at the immensity of meteorological phenomena, at the pleasures of love, none of which appears in the earlier ode, but even these words are paraphrase. The poetry is in the detail, the images, the music, the shifting emotional tones. The two poems are entirely different.

Odes 2. 14, *Eheu fugaces, Postume, Postume*, advises Postumus to enjoy his life in view of the certainty of death, but again the tones are richly different from those of other poems which can be so paraphrased. The battle imagery of the first stanza, the humour of those that follow, the disturbing contrasts between the landscape of life and the landscape of the Underworld, and the painful picture of the fate of Postumus' vintage wine are some of the features which give this poem its power. Modern poetry sometimes displays a welter of sensational but wanton, unconnected images. This poem, by contrast, is rich in metaphor, but the pictures and the concepts are meshed and interactive in a manner which could be called Horace's poetic logic.

Ethics
Odes 2. 16, *Otium divos rogat in patenti prensus Aegaeo*, is in essence a sermon on the Epicurean principle that man can live well on little, but it is a sermon shot through with wit, visualizations, and metaphors. It ends with a statement of Horace's contentment and a definition of his achievement as a poet: to make the native Italian Muse, Camena, into a Greek Camena—to bring to Latin poetry the quality and fame which are the hallmarks of the Greek poetic heritage.

Odes 2. 18, *Non ebur neque aureum mea renidet in domo lacunar* is another sermon on the dangers of wealth and it is lit with those poetic qualities which raised 2. 16 to levels not reached by normal sermons, not least in the picture of the farmer, his wife, and children being driven from their home, and the surrealism of its last three lines.

Poetry
Odes 2. 9, *Non semper imbres nubibus hispidos manant in agros*, is a poem about poetry. There was a literary group in the Augustan circle. Horace's

list of fifteen of the people for whom he writes (*Satires* 1. 10. 81–8) includes the names of Maecenas, Virgil, Pollio, and Valgius. Pollio instituted the practice of public readings, and Horace tells us in *Ars Poetica* 438–44 that his friend Quintilius was a candid critic of what he heard. In accordance with this fashion Horace is here criticizing the elegies of his friend Valgius. He should stop writing doleful poems about the death of the boy he loved and should instead write in praise of the victories of Augustus. Between the two elements in this extraordinary counsel there comes in the third stanza a vivid evocation of one of the most moving passages in Virgil's *Georgics*, followed by two mythological exempla. This progression in which the different elements are linked by repetitions, comparisons, and contrasts, demonstrates characteristic Horatian modulations from topic to topic and tone to tone, and his equally characteristic practice of binding arguments together by imagery and cross-reference within poems.

Odes 2. 13, *Ille et nefasto te posuit die*, starts with a preposterous curse upon some unknown countryman who planted a tree which almost fell on Horace's head on his estate. This is clearly burlesque, but it is followed by a sudden change of tone as Horace reflects that none of us knows from which direction our death will come. Another modulation takes us down into the Underworld to hear Sappho and Alcaeus singing to the attentive shades, and the ode ends, as it began, with burlesque, with a description of some of the most famous mythological denizens of the Underworld. Although this poem touches on poetry, it cannot be taken as a serious statement of Horace's poetic debt to Sappho and Alcaeus. The context is against that, and so, even more decisively, is the unflattering account of Sappho. Here, as in 2. 9, love poetry gets short shrift. Horace, and the audience of the dead, much prefer Alcaeus' poems about war and the expulsion of kings. The main spark of the poem seems to be fun, including the pleasure of parody and the delight in the surreal, but in the midst of this cheerful play he is making it clear, here as elsewhere, that although he often writes in the metre to which Sappho of Lesbos gave her name, he does not share her sentiments and is much more in sympathy with the robustness of Alcaeus.

The gods have not been much in evidence in this book, but in *Odes* 2. 19, *Bacchum in remotis carmina rupibus vidi docentem*, Horace addresses Bacchus and claims that he has seen him teaching Nymphs to sing. In addition to other functions, Bacchus is the god of ecstatic poetry. Hymns addressed to Bacchus are called dithyrambs, and so *Odes* 2. 19 is in some respects a dithyramb. This comes as a surprise because there has been no ecstatic poetry in this book, and because Horace does not normally make such exalted claims for his work. There are, however, two aspects of the poem which are characteristic. It begins and ends cheerfully, like 2. 13. To avoid any risk of boastfulness or owlishness Horace uses humour to prepare the way for lofty claims, and to leave these claims with a smile. Scholars often write of the gods in Horace as though they were empty pasteboard figures, literary devices. The essay on this poem argues that religion means a great deal more than that to this poet.

Odes 2. 20, *Non usitata nec tenui ferar penna*, contains Horace's assertion that he has achieved poetic immortality, and once again his lofty claim is accompanied by burlesque. He mocks at his own pretensions in the first, third, and fourth stanzas in order to render acceptable the exalted claims of the fifth. This is an example of a crucial principle for readers of Horace. He often makes fun of his own devotion to poetry, but there is no doubt about the devotion. On this subject he is not solemn, but he is serious.

THE SOUND

The sound of poetry is part of its essence. Although we do not know exactly how Latin was spoken in Horace's day, the metres he used are well understood and easy to master. Of the twenty odes in this book, twelve are in Alcaics and six in Sapphics, with other metres only in the twelfth and eighteenth odes.

The Sapphic Stanza

Latin metres are based upon the quantity of the syllables. Syllables marked — are long, ˘ short, ~ either long or short. The Sapphic stanza runs as follows

— ˘ — — — | ˘ ˘ — ˘ — ~ (three times)
— ˘ ˘ — ~

There are no variations in this pattern. The template can be laid on any Sapphic stanza and it will fit. Take the last stanza of *Odes* 2. 6:

īllĕ tē mēcūm lŏcŭs ēt bĕātāe
pōstŭlānt ārcēs; ĭb ĭtū călēntēm
dēbĭtā spārgēs lăcrĭmā făvīllām
vātĭs ămīcī.

On the other hand, if the poetry is read aloud or heard in the mind with this pattern uppermost, it will be destroyed. To hear the first line of the

Sapphic as tum-te tum-tum-tum te-te-tum-te-tum-te, is like hearing 'When to the sessions of sweet, silent, thought' as 'When tó the séssions óf sweet sílent thóught'. This is doggerel, not poetry.

The music of Latin poetry requires that each word be spoken with its correct quantities and with its normal accentuation. The word accent falls on the second last syllable if it is long, or if the word has only two syllables, like *lócus*. In longer words, if the second last syllable is short the accent is on the third last. This principle is repeated in long words like *índomitǽque*, *íllacrimábilem*, *enávigánda*. The word accents in *Odes* 2. 6. 21–4 would be heard as follows:

ílle té mécum lócus et beátae
póstulant árces; íbi tú caléntem
débita spárges lácrima favíllam
vátis amíci.

This is not a repetitive jingle, but a counterpoint of variables—the metre, the word accents, the individual sound values, and the dynamic all supporting the shifting nuances of the sense. Our modern punctuation indicates what is obvious and essential. It reminds us that we must read not by lines, but by sense units. There is no pause in the above stanza until *arces*.

In hearing the Sapphic, we should be on the alert for what I have called 'the Sapphic effect'. Every stanza ends with a short fourth line, the Adonius. Rhythm *conveys* no meaning, but it does *affect the impact* of poetry. What follows is subjective. Different readers will hear the poetry of *Odes* 2. 6 differently, but as an example of how the melody may be heard, ask if the Adonius intensifies the sound of a seething sea at *aéstuat únda*, the burden of military service in the one word *mílitiaéque*, the trumping of Greek by Latin as *rúra Phalántho* is followed by *báca Venáfro*, the mere smidgeon of envy that Aulon feels for Falernum at *ínvidet úvis*, and the miracle of the last line of the poem. These effects are intensified as the stanza is rounded off by the regular coincidence of long vowel and word accent not only in the final Adonius but also at the end of the preceding line, *Falérnis ínvidet úvis*.

The Alcaic Stanza

The Alcaic stanza runs as follows:

— — ˘ — — | — ˘ ˘ — ˘ ~
— — ˘ — — | — ˘ ˘ — ˘ ~
— — ˘ — — | — ˘ — ~
— ˘ ˘ — ˘ ˘ | — ˘ — ~

Rhythm depends on repetition. It may help the ear to notice that the first three lines begin in the same way, that the last two end in the same way, as do the first two, and that this ending — ˘ ˘ — ˘ ~ is very like the beginning of the last line. Take as an example the first stanza of *Odes* 2. 14:

eheu fugaces, Postume, Postume,
labuntur anni nec pietas moram
rugis et instanti senectae
adferet indomitaeque morti.

To read the poem with this repetitive rhythm uppermost would be to reduce it to doggerel. The quantities of the syllables must be respected, but the normal accentuation of the words must be heard:

éheu fugáces, Póstume, Póstume,
labúntur ánni nec píetas móram
rúgis et instánti senéctae
ádferet índomitáeque mórti.

In hearing the Alcaic stanza we should be on the alert for 'the Alcaic effect'. The third line of every stanza has two or three short syllables; the fourth line has five or six. So in *Odes* 2. 14 the sense is often intensified by the drag of the third lines and the acceleration of the fourth, notably in lines 3–4 above, and in lines 11–12:

enaviganda sive reges
siv[e] inopes erimus coloni.

[the river which]
we all must cross whether kings
or impoverished tenant farmers.

For other examples of the Alcaic effect, see the Index of Topics.

Elision

Elided vowels are very lightly pronounced and do not contribute to the metre. A final vowel is elided before a word beginning with a vowel, or with -h-: so *siv*[*e*] *inopes* just above, and *nequ*[*e*] *harum*. So too, a final vowel + m, as in *mec*[*um*] *et*.

Take the first stanza of *Odes* 2. 6 in the Sapphic metre. Here the unusual frequency of the elisions and the similarity between the endings of the first two lines add weight to the list of places. Septimius would go anywhere with Horace:

Sēptĭmī, Gādīs ădĭtūrĕ mēc[um] ēt
Cāntăbr[um] īndōctūm iŭgă fērrĕ nōstr[a] ēt
bārbărās Sȳrtēs, ŭbĭ Māură sēmpĕr
  āestŭăt ūndă.

You who would go with me to Gades, Septimius, and
to the Cantabrian, who has never learned to bear our yoke, and
to the barbarian Syrtes, where the Moorish ocean
  for ever boils.

Odes 2. 12 is in **Second Asclepiads**. The five Asclepiadic metres all have a choriamb (— ˘ ˘ —) or choriambs in the middle of the lines. The Second Asclepiadic runs:

— — — ˘ ˘ — — ˘ ˘ — ˘ ~ (three times)
— — — ˘ ˘ — ˘ ~

Odes 2. 18 is in **Hipponacteans**:

— ˘ — ˘ — ˘ — ˘ ~
˘ — ˘ — ~ — ˘ — ˘ — ~

nōn ĕbūr nĕqu[e] āurĕūm
mĕā rĕnīdĕt īn dŏmō lăcūnār

This is how this metre is printed, as four trochaic feet + one syllable, alternating with five iambic feet + one syllable. On the other hand, the Romans declaimed their verse, and silent reading was not the usual practice. So this presentation, though convenient for scribes and printers, is not how the metre would have been heard. The presenting pattern would have been lines of nine trochees:

nōn ĕbūr nĕqu[e] āurĕūm mĕā rĕnīdĕt īn dŏmō lăcūnār

This suggestion is borne out by the large number of short lines which run on unbroken into the longer lines. Read in this way the metre gives no impression of being a combination of two different rhythms. It is simply a long string of trochees, eminently suitable for hammering home a sermon. In this respect it resembles Horace's epodes. Many of these too are devoted to sermonizing, and most of them are written with short and long lines alternating, but in unbroken iambics, not, as here, in unbroken trochees.

If this poem were declaimed according to its metre, we would hear a procession of 180 trochees, and could not endure it. The trochees are the under-rhythm. The variety and energy of the verse comes with the word accents, as they stress *ébur*, *aúreum*, and *méa* and encourage the reader to contrast Horace's own house with the ostentatious palaces he is satirizing:

non ébur nequ[e] aúreum méa renídet in dómo lacúnar

Accentual Iambics and Trochees

The interplay of verse rhythm and word accent is part of the unmeasurable effect of poetry, but sometimes there occurs a series of repeated word accents which unmistakably intensify the sense of the words by setting up striking iambic (te-tum) or trochaic (tum-te) rhythms. The probative example is the opening of the fourth book of the *Odes*:

> íntermíssa, Vénus, díu
> rúrsus bélla móves? párce, précor, précor.
> nón sum quális éram bónae
> sub regno Cinarae.

> Back to war, Venus, after all
> these years? Spare me, spare me, I beg you.
> I'm not the man I was
> in good Cinara's reign.

The metre is an alternation of the two lines used in the Second Asclepiad (see above on 2. 12), but the first three lines consist of fourteen accentual trochees as marked.

No such spectacular effect occurs in Book 2 but readers can test whether this technique of reading adds to the force of *Odes* 2. 5. 13–14, 11. 5–6, 12. 1, and 13. 27–8. (See too West 1995*c*: 106 on *Odes* 3. 9. 9–10).

Such repeated rhythms are important in hexameter poetry also, in Virgil's *Aeneid*, for instance, and Horace's *Satires*. Consider only *Satires* 1. 6. 45–6:

> nunc ad me redeo libertino patre natum,
> quem rodunt omnes libertino patre natum.

> Now I come back to my own case, the freedman's son
> they all sneer at because I'm a freedman's son.

I have argued on page xi that this makes sense as a schoolboys' gibe. We can hear them chanting it, not 'Cówardy, cówardy cústard', but *ródunt ómnes líbertíno pátre nátum.*

THE TEXT

The text printed is the Oxford Classical Text by E. C. Wickham in its second edition by H. W. Garrod (1912) with variations as follows:

5. 16 petit]petet
10. 8 saepius]saevius
11. 23 in comptum]incomptum
13. 23 discriptas]descriptas
17. 14 Gyas]Gyges
18. 36 revexit]revinxit

Odes Book 2

I

Motum ex Metello consule civicum
bellique causas et vitia et modos
ludumque Fortunae gravisque
principum amicitias et arma

nondum expiatis uncta cruoribus,
periculosae plenum opus aleae,
tractas, et incedis per ignis
suppositos cineri doloso.

paulum severae Musa tragoediae
desit theatris: mox ubi publicas
res ordinaris, grande munus
Cecropio repetes cothurno,

insigne maestis praesidium reis
et consulenti, Pollio, curiae,
cui laurus aeternos honores
Delmatico peperit triumpho.

iam nunc minaci murmure cornuum
perstringis auris, iam litui strepunt,
iam fulgor armorum fugaces
terret equos equitumque vultus.

audire magnos iam videor duces
non indecoro pulvere sordidos,
et cuncta terrarum subacta
praeter atrocem animum Catonis.

Iuno et deorum quisquis amicior
Afris inulta cesserat impotens
tellure victorum nepotes
rettulit inferias Iugurthae.

quis non Latino sanguine pinguior
campus sepulcris impia proelia
testatur auditumque Medis
Hesperiae sonitum ruinae?

I

The civil disturbance which began in the consulship of Metellus,
the causes of the war, its evils and the ways of it,
the play of Fortune, the fatal friendships
of the great, and armour smeared

with still unexpiated blood—a work fraught
with the hazard of the dice—all these you take in hand,
stepping over fires smouldering
under the treacherous ash.

For a little let your stern tragic Muse desert
the theatre; in due course when you have set
the affairs of state in order, you will return
to your great duty in Cecrops' tragic boot,

a glorious bulwark for the abject defendant
and for the Senate consulting you, Pollio,
for whom the laurel brought forth honours
ever green in your Dalmatian triumph.

But now you grate upon our ears with the menacing murmur
of horns; now bugles are blaring and the dazzle
of armour is now putting fear into fleeing horses
and the faces of horsemen.

I seem now to hear of great leaders
begrimed with honourable dust
and the whole world subdued
except the fierce spirit of Cato.

Powerless, Juno and all the gods who favour Africa
had abandoned it and left it unavenged,
but now they have given the descendants of the victors
as offerings to the shade of Jugurtha.

What field is not fattened with Italian blood,
its graves testifying to impious battles
and the fall of Hesperia
heard by the Medes?

qui gurges aut quae flumina lugubris
ignara belli? quod mare Dauniae
non decoloravere caedes?
quae caret ora cruore nostro?

sed ne relictis, Musa procax, iocis
Ceae retractes munera neniae,
mecum Dionaeo sub antro
quaere modos leviore plectro.

At the beginning of the first satire in his second book, Horace pretends to consult Trebatius, explaining that if he does not write satire he cannot sleep. Trebatius' reply is that those who cannot sleep should swim the Tiber three times (we take it he means six) and make sure they are awash with wine in the evening. This is amusing enough, but the poem comes spectacularly to life because we are lucky enough to have Cicero's letters *Ad Familiares* 7. 6–22, where we learn that C. Trebatius Testa, whom Horace was pretending to consult, was (*a*) a distinguished jurisconsult; (*b*) a keen swimmer; (*c*) not averse to an evening's drinking; (*d*) teaser and teased throughout the surviving correspondence with Cicero.

The satire cannot be understood unless we know about the character and interests of the addressee. It is *ad hominem* poetry. So are many of the odes in the second book. Of the twenty poems in Book 2, thirteen are addressed to living individuals and 'are naturally coloured by the interests and ethos of the addressee' (Nisbet and Hubbard 1978: 2). This first ode of the book is addressed in line 14 to Pollio. We shall therefore ask how much Pollio there is in the poem.

C. Asinius Pollio was born in 76 BC, and fought by the side of Caesar throughout the Civil Wars from 49 to 45 BC, serving as his legate in Africa and Spain. On Caesar's assassination in 44, he transferred his allegiance to Antony, was consul in 40, and won a triumph over the Parthini in 39. He then retired from military life and devoted himself to literature, notably his history of the Civil War, and used the spoils of his triumph to establish the first national library in Rome. He distanced himself from Antony after he became embroiled with Cleopatra—Pollio never saw the queen—and Velleius Paterculus, 2. 86. 3, preserves the characteristically pungent words with which he responded to Octavian's request that he

This ode contains a large number of historical allusions, which are summarized in a chronological table at the end of this essay.

What sea, what rivers, have not known
this sorry war? What ocean has not been stained
by the slaughter of Daunians? What shore
is not soaked with our blood?

But come, my naughty Muse, do not leave
your cheerful ways to undertake the duties of the Cean dirge,
but stay with me in Dione's cave
and look for measures for a lighter plectrum.

should sail with him to the war which led to the battle of Actium: 'My services to Antony have been too great; his generosity to me is too well known: I shall therefore keep out of your quarrel and will be the spoils of the victor', *mea in Antonium maiora merita sunt, illius in me beneficia notiora; itaque discrimini vestro me subtraham et ero praeda victoris*. He died in AD 4.

The first two stanzas of the poem clearly celebrate Pollio's lost *Historiae*, and Nisbet and Hubbard's great commentary provides proof that the dry content and somewhat prosaic language of these stanzas mimic the opening chapters of ancient historians, and sometimes Pollio's own *Historiae*: Roman historians often give their starting-date in terms of the consuls of the day; historians Greek and Roman claim to search for the causes and descant upon the evils of wars; the ways, *modos*, of war as opposed to its causes, *causas*, the how as opposed to the why, is a distinction drawn for instance by Tacitus in *Historiae* 1. 4. 1; the sport of Fortune is a common theme; the burdensome friendships of the great, burdensome to the great and to their followers and to the whole Roman world, point firmly to Pollio's starting-point, the alliance of 60 BC between Caesar and Pompey; in saying that Pollio's work is full of the dangerous die, *periculosae plenum opus aleae*, Horace is not exaggerating. Pliny the Younger tells us in his *Letters* (5. 8. 12) that in writing contemporary history grave offence can be given and little favour is to be expected, *graves offensae levis gratia*. The hazard was particularly high for Pollio, Antony's man who had refused to fight for Octavian. He knew that Octavian would be reading his account of the Civil War with some care. But the relevance of line 6 is sharpened by the wording. Pollio crossed the Rubicon with Caesar in 49 BC when Caesar quoted Menander, *anerriphtho kubos*, 'Let the die be cast', a phrase which became proverbial in Latin as *iacta alea est*. Pollio may have been standing on the river bank at Caesar's side and heard him saying it. He certainly would not have failed to render it into Latin in his *Historiae*. This line in Horace is an inescapable allusion, nicely turned. The risk for Caesar was that he was marching on his native city; the risk for Pollio is that having been a lieutenant of Antony, he is now writing a history under Augustus. Having been a staunch upholder of the republic (he used his spoils of war also to rebuild the Hall of Liberty, *Atrium Libertatis*, at the foot of the Capitol) he is now writing history during the principate. The buildings of Rome frequently caught fire (lines 7–8) and people might walk over the ashes thinking there was no longer any danger. But there was. We know that Augustus established his regime and maintained it till he died in his bed in AD 14, but Horace could not know that. At the beginning of 23 BC Augustus was critically ill, and late in the same year his nephew Marcellus, who might have succeeded him, died at the age of 20. There was unrest in the air, culminating in the trial of Antonius Primus and the conspiracy of Caepio and Murena (see Crook, 84–8). These were dangerous times.

In the third stanza Horace leaves historiography and turns to Pollio's other accomplishments. First he is complimented on his tragedies: they will be missed while he writes history; they perform a great service, *grande munus*, and the noun may refer not only to political duty but also to plays, *munera theatralia*. Horace speaks as poet to poet, perhaps feeling that tragedy is a higher form than history, perhaps also remembering Aristotle's reasoning, that tragedy deals with the general, and history only with the particular (*The Art of Poetry* 1451^{b}). There is a difficulty in lines 10–11 where Horace talks of the writing of history in terms of ordering the affairs of state, *ubi res publicas ordinaris*. But Pollio is only describing the ordering of the state, not ordering it. The grandiose formulation is a form of flattery, not unlike the effect of the verb *tractas*, 'you handle' in line 7, where Pollio seems to be 'handling' weapons smeared with blood, when he is only describing the use of them. So too in line 17 Pollio is said to be a horn-player, but we know he is reading from his *Historiae*. The whole tone of the references to tragedy in the third stanza is elevated. Two of the three words in line 12 are Greek, *Cecropio* alluding to Cecrops, the legendary founder-king of Athens, and *cothurno*, a poetic singular, being the buskin, the high boot of the Athenian tragic actor. In line 13 Pollio is praised for his work in the courts and there is evidence to support the terms of the praise. Quintilian (10. 1. 113) and Tacitus (*Dialogus* 25. 3) both have a high regard for his oratory, and we know the titles of nine of Pollio's speeches and eight of them are for the defence. Lines 13–14 bring another difficulty. They say that the Senate consults Pollio, whereas technically the Senate does not consult, it is the magistrate who consults the Senate. Scholars have therefore taken *consulenti* as standing for *consilianti*, making Pollio a bulwark for the Senate *debating*. But this is surely to blunt the edge of flattery. In 23 BC Pollio was 53 years old, a senior and distinguished member of the Senate, a consular and a *triumphator*, to whom younger members would show deference. Horace is offering praise with a tinge of exaggeration as he did in lines 10–11, *res publicas ordinaris*. The last two lines of the stanza tell us that he was a *triumphator* for his victories in 39 BC over the Parthini who had assisted Pompey before Pharsalus, and even here there may be a diplomatic slant. The Parthini lived around Dyrrachium on the north-western seaboard of Greece, within the jurisdiction of Antony, and Pollio defeated them as legate under Antony. The Dalmatians, *Delmati*, whose territory, Illyricum, began 40 miles to the north, came within the remit of Octavian by the terms of the Treaty of Brundisium, and their land was the scene of successful campaigns by Octavian in operations beginning in 35 BC. By referring to Pollio's triumph over the Parthini as a Dalmatian triumph, Horace is perhaps drawing a veil over a military success of Antony's, confusing it with the subsequent successes of Octavian. For an important discussion of this vexed problem, see Woodman (1983) on Velleius 2. 78. 2.

At line 17 we return to Pollio's *Historiae*. Ancient rhetorical theory valued vividness in historical narrative, *enargeia*, *repraesentatio*, the power to bring actions vividly before the mind's eye of the reader or listener. Without warning, with a suddenness which sharpens the *repraesentatio*, Horace finds himself seeing and hearing the events of the Civil Wars and conveys their immediacy by quadruple anaphora of *iam*, 'now' and a rush of sensory stimuli. 'Horns' and 'bugles' are of necessity an approximate translation. The essential point is that the *litui* shrill, *strepunt*, and their pitch is contrasted with the deeper note, *murmure*, of the horns. By a similar, characteristically Horatian contrast the battle starts with the glitter of armour and ends with leaders begrimed with dust in line 22. Even more vivid is the picture in 19–20 where the flash of the armour terrifies horses and makes them take to flight, *fugaces terret equos*, and also, by a startling zeugma, terrifies the faces of the horsemen. Wilkinson (91) is reminded of the white face of Darius and his Persians pursued by Alexander as shown in the Pompeian mosaic in the museum at Naples. We are bound to ask what particular battle, if any, is described in this stanza, and the answer is not far to seek. Before the decisive defeat of Pompey at Pharsalus in Thessaly in 48 BC, when Caesar's 1,000 battle-hardened cavalrymen were faced by 5,000 of the enemy, in his harangue before the battle Caesar ordered them to depart from standard tactics and strike at the faces of the opposing riders, 'in the hopes that young gentlemen, who had not known much of battles and wounds, but came wearing their hair long, in the flower of their age and height of their beauty, would be apprehensive of such blows, and not care for hazarding both a danger at present and a blemish for the future' (Plutarch, *Caesar* 45. 2 in Dryden's translation revised by Arthur Hugh Clough). Pollio fought at Pharsalus under Caesar, and Pollio seems to have been an important source for Plutarch. (See Pelling, 27.)

If that fifth stanza evokes Pharsalus, the sixth moves forward in time to the defeat of the Pompeians at Thapsus in 46, after which Cato committed suicide rather than continue to live under Caesar. In that campaign Plutarch (*Caesar* 52) tells us that Pollio and Caesar fought side by side, and Caesar and his lieutenants were not behind the lines at staff headquarters but in the thick of battle. Pollio will not have omitted to describe the moment which seemed to mark the end of the Civil Wars when Caesar and his staff officers met together after the battle begrimed with dust and sweat, but victorious, hence *non indecoro pulvere sordidos*. Another *repraesentatio* is the reference to the whole of the world subjected to Caesar. The contemporary Roman would know that after the battle of Thapsus the Senate had voted to Caesar a statue with a globe at, or under, his feet, as discussed by Weinstock (41–51).

The obvious difficulty about these suggestions is that lines 10–11 make it clear that Pollio's history is not yet written. The simplest response to that objection would be to posit that Pollio and others talked freely in Rome about their war experiences, but there is another possibility. Pollio was the first Roman to issue invitations to readings of his works and Horace could easily have heard him performing some of his work in progress. The strange wording in line 21, 'I seem to hear', *audire . . . videor*, literally 'I am seen to hear' now leaps into light. Horace is not imagining these scenes directly, but imagining the voice of Pollio declaiming his account of these scenes—'I seem to hear that the leaders were begrimed with dust and all the world subject to Caesar.' Into this stanza of praise for Pollio's part in the battle of Thapsus and for his account of it in his *Historiae*, Horace has insinuated a passing allusion to the *recitatio* by invitation, this innovation of Pollio's which was of such importance for the subsequent development of Latin literature. We think of reading. The Romans thought of hearing works read. There is, however, a much easier way to interpret line 21. For *audire* read *videre*, 'I seem to see', and scholars have emended the text accordingly. This is much smoother and well suits the *repraesentatio*, but Horace is not always smooth. The emendation is not so meaningful as the manuscript reading. It does not hint how Horace knows what is in the unpublished *Historiae*, and it removes the subtle allusion to Pollio's famous innovation.

We stay in Africa in lines 25–8 as Horace gives a vivid picture of the defeated gods leaving the land they loved. Juno, according to a later story told by Macrobius, 3. 9. 7, had been summoned out of Carthage by the Romans at the end of the Third Punic War in 146 BC by the ceremony of *evocatio*, as discussed by Fraenkel (237–9). The sequence is clear. The gods had abandoned, *cesserat*, Carthage in 146 BC when the city was destroyed by Scipio Africanus Minor. Then Jugurtha, king of neighbouring Numidia, surrendered to Marius and was executed after Marius' triumph on the first day of 104 BC. In 46 BC an army led by Q. Metellus Pius Scipio, a member of the family of that same Scipio Africanus Minor, the conqueror of Carthage a hundred years before, was defeated by Caesar at Thapsus, a town in that same part of North Africa. Horace is adding to the horror of the Civil Wars by imagining that this slaughter of Romans by Romans at Thapsus was an offering to the shade of Jugurtha and divine revenge wreaked upon the conquerors of Carthage. There is a little awkwardness here in that, in accordance with Macrobius' story, Juno would have transferred her affections from Carthage to Rome after the successful *evocatio* in 146 BC. But this is a small price for Horace to pay in order to darken his account of the Civil Wars by involving the anger of the gods.

The allusions to the Civil War have moved from the consulship of Metellus in 60 BC to Pharsalus in north Greece in 48, and to Thapsus in Africa in 46. Even without mentioning the battles at Ilerda in 49 and Munda in Spain in 45, Horace may fairly ask in lines 29–31 what field does not testify to impious battles fought by Romans against Romans. Nor is he exaggerating when he says in line 31 that the Medes have heard the sound of the collapse of the Roman world. This brings us down to 42 BC and the battle of Philippi, where Antony and Octavian defeated Cassius and Brutus. Encouraged, no doubt, by the news of this disastrous battle, and abetted by Cassius' lieutenant Labienus, the Parthians defeated a Roman army led by Decidius Saxa and overran Syria in 41–40 BC. This ode not only alludes throughout to Pollio's *Historiae*, but also serves as a record of Pollio's distinguished career during these troubled times. After crossing the Rubicon with Caesar in 49 BC, he fought beside him at Pharsalia in 48, at Thapsus in 46, and at Munda in 45.

The passionate denunciation of civil war which comes in the next stanza is also likely to have been a feature of Pollio's history. Such sentiments would accord exactly with remarks he made in the three surviving letters he wrote to Cicero in the dark days of 43 BC. 'My own nature and my interests draw me to a love of peace and of liberty' (*Ad Fam.* 10. 31. 2). 'You must therefore think of me firstly as a man whose desire is for peace (for I simply want every citizen of Rome to be safe)' (10. 31. 5). 'If, therefore, there is anyone who takes delight in present events, because both the commanders and the veterans on Caesar's side appear to have perished, yet they must after that mourn when they look at the devastation of Italy' (10. 33. 1). These remarks of Pollio are of course coloured by the situation and the addressee, but everything in his future career, his determined withdrawal from military service and from civil strife, which he succeeded in maintaining despite the sharpness of his tongue, his devoted pursuit of his own literary work, and his encouragement of the work of others, testifies to his hatred of war and his love of peace and of the arts of peace. It tells us something about the man that he was on terms with Catullus, Calvus, Cinna, Gallus, Virgil, and now Horace. The relevant details here, as ever, are to be found in Nisbet and Hubbard's commentary (1978: 8; see also Courtney, 254–6).

If the sentiments in this great second last stanza are the sentiments of Pollio, they are also the sentiments of Horace, and he has conveyed that by the word 'Daunian'. We are familiar with the wide variety of proper names available to Latin versifiers—Virgil uses half a dozen words for Italians—but Daunia is the remote, wild, area in the south-east of Italy and it is chosen here because it includes the town of Venusia where Horace was born. He is thinking of the men of his own town and district. Readers of Latin are all familiar with the ascending tricolon with anaphora, three cola each larger than the one before and each introduced by the same word. Horace's grief at the slaughter of the Civil War bears such an emphasis that it calls for a *descending* tetracolon with quasi-anaphora of *quis*, *qui*, *quae*, *quod*, *quae*. *Quis campus* takes up the whole of the stanza 29–32. The next colon, including *qui* and *quae*, demands eight words, *quod mare* six, and finally *quae caret ora cruore nostro* has only five short words, but yet is a resounding climax. Even after the astonishing sound effects of alliteration and assonance in the weighty third line of the Alcaic stanza, *non decoloravere caedes*, the greatest horror comes in the assertion in the final line that every shore in the Mediterranean has Roman blood on it, a statement rendered even more poignant by the tripping lightness of the short syllables, the two successive accented long syllables -or-, the four long -o- syllables in the last seven, three of them bearing the word accent, *quae caret óra cruóre nóstro?* Add to all these vowel effects the snarl of the five occurrences of the dog's letter -r-, *littera canina* as Persius calls it at *Satires* 1. 109–10, and the horror can be heard.

In the minds of Romans in 23 BC the greatest naval battle of all the Civil War period was the most recent, the battle of Actium in 31 BC at which the sea grew red with slaughter according to Virgil, *caede rubescunt* at *Aeneid* 8. 695, and dyed with blood, *cruore infectum*, according to Seneca, *De Clementia* 1. 11. 1. The chronological sweep of the Civil Wars, which began in the first line with 60 BC, has ended at the battle of Actium in 31. On the other hand, Nisbet and Hubbard have thoroughly assessed the historical allusions in the poem and decided that its most likely date of composition was 34 BC, three years before the battle of Actium, and that therefore the blood that discoloured the sea was blood shed in the sea battles against Sextus Pompeius in 37–36 BC. But the dating of Horace's odes is a complex matter. We await any refutation of the view that these three books of poems were issued in 23 BC (on all this question, see Nisbet and Hubbard 1970: pp. xxvii–xxxvii). But we also know that Horace was working on the collection for more than a decade before that date. On his own admission, he thought it was a good idea to keep a poem in the drawer for more than eight years, on the grounds that what is not published can be deleted, *nonumque prematur in annum . . . delere licebit quod non edideris* (*Ars Poetica* 388–90). He would not have issued a poem in 23 BC in ignorance of the political situation in that year. Therefore, allusions to an event before 23 BC are not proof that the whole poem in which they occur was written in the year of the event, only that the lines in which they occur were written after the event. Parts of some odes are set in earlier years, but Horace's final viewpoint is from the year of publication, and here, when he says that every sea has been stained by Daunian blood, for him and for his contemporary readers that must include the sea off Actium. On this approach, all the odes of these first three books are to be read as poems of 23 BC.

Every stanza in this poem has alluded to, or at least been in harmony with, what must have been in the *Historiae* of Pollio. Now, in the last four lines, Horace bids his Muse to leave such grievous topics as would have deserved treatment by Simonides of Ceos (famous for his dirges and epitaphs), and devote himself to cheerful poetry and the poetry of love (Dione in line 39 being a name of Venus in Latin poetry). Here commentators sometimes say that Horace is turning away from Pollio to himself. Syndikus, for instance, believes that Horace thinks no more of Pollio in stanzas 7–10. But is Horace turning away from Pollio? Surely the unity of this poem and its power depend upon the sympathy which Horace shows throughout for the career, ideals, and achievements of his addressee. Pollio fought for Caesar and Antony and then determinedly declined to take any further part in the quarrels of the great, preferring to devote his life to the law, the politics of the Senate, and most of all to literature, to history and tragedy, to his library and *recitationes* and literary friends. Horace fought for the conspirators at Philippi against Antony and Octavian and perhaps against Pollio (Velleius, 2. 63. 2). He then returned to Rome and spent his life as a poet and a member of the Augustan establishment. Both men had known war and anguish of conscience. Both were survivors and enjoyed the benefits of peace. The last stanza of this ode is not only about Horace. It also asserts the resemblances between Horace and Pollio. In stating his own choice, Horace is obliquely commending the choice made by Pollio. Pollio, too, wrote love poetry (Pliny, *Letters* 5. 3. 5).

There is a third important player. What did Augustus make of this? Here is an Augustan court poet, who had fought against Octavian/Augustus, opening a book of verse with deep sympathy and praise for a man who had fought for Antony and declined to fight for Octavian, who was famed for his frankness and independence of mind. It would be possible to hunt the poem for veiled criticism of Augustus. Do the quarrels of lines 3–4 include Augustus' involvement in the Second Triumvirate? Do lines 5–8 hint at vindictiveness on the part of Augustus? Does line 14 suggest that the Senate needs Pollio's protection against Augustus? Does the praise of the republican saint in line 24 constitute an attack upon the principate? Does the reference to Actium at 34–6 involve Augustus in guilt for the horrors of the Civil Wars? Any of these questions could be debated, but they are all superficial and insensitive. *Concordia* and *Clementia* were vital planks in the Augustan settlement. The odes to Plancus and Sestius in the first book, and in the second the ode to Pompeius, 2. 7, demonstrate that Augustus wished to pardon all those who had opposed his rise (except the slayers of Julius Caesar, who would never find forgiveness) and who were willing to accept the new regime. But for this, Horace and perhaps Pollio would have been dead before the battle of Actium. The settlement also claimed that the republic had been restored and that this was now a Golden Age. One of its slogans is represented on the Shield of Virtue, *Clupeus Virtutis*, presented to Augustus by the Senate and people of Rome in 27 BC for his courage, clemency, justice, and piety. A civilized tolerance was part of the ambience in the early 30s and in so far as this poem is celebrating that dispensation, it is praise of Augustus. This is a far more sensible explanation of its tone than any notion that Horace was biting the hand that fed him, was conniving with Pollio to criticize the Princeps and hoping he did not notice. Augustus would have noticed.

Table of Events Relevant to Odes *2.1*

146 BC	End of Third Punic War. Carthage defeated by Scipio Africanus Minor. By the rite of *evocatio*, Juno called upon to abandon Carthage (see lines 25–6).
104	Jugurtha, king of Numidia, defeated by Marius and executed (lines 27–8).
76	Birth of C. ASINIUS POLLIO, historian, tragedian, orator, initiator of *recitationes*, founder of the first open library in Rome, and lover of peace (see Cicero, *Ad Fam.* 10. 31 and 33).
60	Caesar allies with Pompey (lines 1–4).
49	Caesar crosses the Rubicon (line 6).
49–45	Civil War.
48	Caesar's veterans defeat the aristocratic youths of Rome at Pharsalus (lines 19–20).
46	After the defeat of the republicans at Thapsus under Q. Metellus Scipio, Cato kills himself rather than live under Caesar (line 24). At the end of the battle Caesar and his lieutenants meet on a hillock (lines 21–2) and salute the end of civil war. Then the Senate vote Caesar a statue with the globe at or under his feet (line 23).
44	Caesar assassinated, Pollio switches allegiance to Antony.
41–40	Parthians defeat a Roman army under Decidius Saxa and overrun Syria (lines 31–2).
40	Pollio consul.
39	Pollio celebrates triumph over the Parthini in Illyria (lines 15–16).
	Pollio distances himself from Antony when the latter becomes embroiled with Cleopatra.
32–31	Pollio declines to support Octavian at Actium.
23	Pollio 53 years old. Horace, *Odes* 1–3 appear.
AD 4	Pollio dies.

II

NULLUS argento color est avaris
abdito terris, inimice lamnae
Crispe Sallusti, nisi temperato
  splendeat usu.

vivet extento Proculeius aevo,
notus in fratres animi paterni;
illum aget penna metuente solvi
  Fama superstes.

latius regnes avidum domando
spiritum, quam si Libyam remotis
Gadibus iungas et uterque Poenus
  serviat uni.

crescit indulgens sibi dirus hydrops,
nec sitim pellit, nisi causa morbi
fugerit venis et aquosus albo
  corpore languor.

redditum Cyri solio Phraaten
dissidens plebi numero beatorum
eximit Virtus, populumque falsis
  dedocet uti

vocibus, regnum et diadema tutum
deferens uni propriamque laurum,
quisquis ingentis oculo irretorto
  spectat acervos.

Ancient poets often received financial and material support from wealthy individuals and repaid it with poems. These might contain naked flattery, as displayed in a Greek epigram in which Crinagoras of Mitylene addressed this same C. Sallustius Crispus, an extremely wealthy member of the equestrian class who was to succeed Maecenas as chief adviser to Augustus. Crinagoras plays upon the fact that there was a shrine to the *Tres Fortunae*, the Three Fortunes, near the sumptuous Horti Sallustiani which Sallustius had inherited from his great-uncle, the historian Sallust.

II

Silver has no colour while hidden
in the greedy earth. You are no lover of metal,
Crispus Sallustius, unless it shines
  in tempered use.

Proculeius will live on to distant ages,
renowned for his fatherly feeling for his brothers.
His fame will survive and carry him on wings
  that scorn to droop.

You can rule a broader kingdom by subduing greed
in your heart than by joining Libya
to distant Cadiz, and making both Carthages
  slaves to one man.

The dreaded dropsy swells by self-indulgence.
It does not quench its thirst till what causes the disease
takes flight from the veins, and watery languor
  leaves the pallid body.

Phraates is restored to the throne of Cyrus,
but Virtue dissents from the mob and excludes him
from the roll of the truly rich. She teaches
  the people not to use false

words, and grants a secure kingdom and diadem
and inalienable laurel to that man alone
who sees heaped-up wealth
  and gives it not a backward glance.

To match the deep wealth of your heart, Crispus Sallustius,
  you ought to have as neighbours not only the Three Fortunes,
but all the Fortunes there are. For what shall suffice such a man
  to further the infinite happiness of his friends?
But now let Caesar, who is greater than Fortunes, grant
  you increase. Without him what Fortune is secure?

(*Palatine Anthology* 16. 40)

This is praise of Sallustius' bounty in a witty dress, and the last two lines economically include praise of the infinite bounty of Augustus.

Praise from Pindar comes at a different level of sophistication and of poetry:

> If you have any desire to win sweet praise eternally,
> weary not in spending, but spread sail to the wind
> like a steersman, and be not misled, dear friend,
> by easy profits. When men are dead and gone,
> only the glory which survives them proclaims
> the manner of their lives to chroniclers and poets.
> The generous virtue of Croesus does not die.
>
> (*Pythian* 1. 90–4)

After direct praise of Hieron, king of Syracuse, Pindar lavishes his advice, and supports it by bold imagery, exalted language, and proud assertion of the imperishable value of his art, appending a proverbial example of wealth and generosity.

Horace is less obvious and more complex. He celebrates the patronage provided by Sallustius without mentioning it, but by castigating meanness in the first stanza and praising an example of generosity in the second. The implication is that Sallustius himself is not mean, but generous. In the third Horace argues that it is better to check one's own acquisitiveness than own vast estates. The implication is that Sallustius has not been acquisitive. A second example follows, this time from medicine. Horace does not say dully that acquisitiveness is like the dropsy, but simply plunges into the example and leaves us to observe and imagine the resemblances. Dropsy swells until the patient stops indulging himself with water. The implication is that Sallustius does not indulge himself by the insatiable accumulation of wealth. The final example is the restoration of Phraates to the throne of Parthia. His apparent success is in fact a failure because it is not approved by Virtue. The implication is that Sallustius is virtuous. Nothing has been expressly said about Sallustius, but it is easy to catch the drift.

The poem is weighed down with philosophy. It is, for example, a little unfair to accuse the earth of greed because it hides unmined silver and does not put it to use. Puzzling also is *lamna*, literally 'sheet metal'. Sallustius is said to be 'hostile to sheet metal unless it shines with tempered use'. The puzzle is that sheet metal could not be used, that is spent, until it ceased to be sheet metal and was made into coins. I take it that Horace is mimicking the portentous tones of the philosophical preacher who would not soil his lips by mentioning money, but describes it for what it is, namely discs of sheet metal, a turn of speech which later passes into the vulgar language of *nouveaux riches* as in Petronius 57. 4 and 58. 8. The mention of 'tempered use' is preacher's word play. In arguing for the temperate use of metal Horace plays with the idea of the use of tempered metal like the bronze in Pliny, *Natural History* 7. 197, *aes temperatum*. In this *ad hominem* poetry we may smile at the pun, remembering, as Horace's contemporaries would, that Sallust owned copper mines in the Valle d'Aosta and even gave his name to a high-grade copper, *aes Sallustianum*, praised by Pliny in his *Natural History* 34. 3.

Greek and Roman orators, poets, and philosophers, like Pindar, loved to argue from examples, *exempla*. The first in this poem is a story about Proculeius, brother of Maecenas' wife Terentia, and like Sallustius a trusted agent of Augustus. It was Proculeius who climbed a ladder to break into the mausoleum where the doomed Cleopatra had taken refuge and seized the dagger from her, a story alluded to in Horace, *Odes* 1. 37. He is known to posterity for his generosity to poets (Juvenal, 7. 94), but Horace is too subtle to mention that. Instead he receives ringing paradoxical praise for his fatherly care for his brothers, according to the ancient commentator for sharing his fortune with them after they had been ruined by the Civil Wars. There is some density of implication in this stanza. First, Sallustius is praised, tacitly, by association. Second, Horace has succeeded in one ode in honouring two important figures in the entourage of Augustus. He has played similar tricks already in 1. 6 and 24 and Crinagoras has done the same in the poem translated at the beginning of this note. Third, in line 5 where, literally, 'Proculeius will live on in extended time', this extension is linked with the broader kingdom, *Latius regnes*, at the beginning of the next stanza.

Here the Stoic flavour is confirmed by the emphasis upon the need to subdue desire and also by the allusion to true kingship. This is conveyed in the references to ruling, subduing, and enslaving, *regnes*, *domando*, and *serviat*, a Stoic image which will recur in the last two stanzas. Horace himself assures us that the Stoic sage

uno minor est Iove, dives,
liber, honoratus, pulcher, rex denique regum,
praecipue sanus, nisi cum pituita molesta est.

(*Epistles* 1. 1. 106–8)

is second only to Jupiter, wealthy,
free, honoured, beautiful, king indeed of kings,
and above all healthy, except when he has a nasty cold.

In the ode Horace bends this maxim to his argument by comparing the conquest of desire, not to the conquest of kingdoms, but to the mania of Roman landowners for increasing their holdings by joining up their properties, *continuando agros*, as condemned at *Odes* 3. 16. 42. Pliny in his *Natural History* 18. 35 tells us that in the time of Nero half of Africa was owned by six landlords. This same practice is satirized by Petronius in *Satiricon* 48. 3, where Trimalchio, speaking in Cumae on the Bay of Naples, wants to add Sicily to his own little place so that he can sail through his estate when he fancies going to Africa. The satire here in Horace is less extreme. There were many Carthaginian settlements along the south coast of Spain, from Gades, modern Cadiz, west of the Strait of Gibraltar to Nova Carthago at the south-east tip of the peninsula (Strabo, 3. 149). To join all that to Carthage in Libya would make an estate to gladden the heart even of Trimalchio.

In the next stanza 'the ugly description of dropsy . . . reflects the plain-spoken parables of diatribe' according to Nisbet and Hubbard, where diatribe refers to the bruising style of popular sermonizing on ethical subjects associated particularly with the Cynic and Stoic schools of philosophy. Bion actually includes this analogy in a fragment recorded by Teles on page 39 of Hense's edition of his diatribe 'On Poverty and Wealth'. The disease is vividly, almost audibly, personified as a monster, perhaps the dreaded water-snake, the Hydra, gorging itself on water, and never sated. A typically Horatian contrast between blood and water lends tension to the symptomology in lines 15–16, where *albo*, *causa*, *aquosus*, *venis* interact to make us understand that the *pallor* of the patient is *caused* by the *water* in the *veins*.

So far every stanza has been self-contained, each punctuated in most editions as a separate sentence. Now the ode moves to its climax in praise of Augustus' foreign policy, which demands two stanzas linked by the striking enjambement of *vocibus*, Virtue, 'the people *false* unteaches to use | *words*', where *vocibus* is separated from its adjective *falsis*, and is not only in a new line, but even in a new stanza. In English this is gibberish but the case-endings of Latin have allowed the poet to put his words in the most expressive order without fear of being misunderstood. We wait in some suspense to hear what it is that is false. (See Index of Topics, under Hyperbaton.)

The allusion is to Tiridates' second rebellion against Phraates IV, king of Parthia. There can be little doubt that Tiridates was a puppet used by Augustus to unsettle the Parthian regime. After his first attempt, he was allowed by Augustus to settle in Syria in 29 BC. After the failure of his second, about five years later, he fled to Augustus in Spain, taking Phraates' son with him. Augustus in his *Res Gestae* 32 describes this débâcle as follows: 'The following kings sought refuge with me as suppliants: Tiridates, King of Parthia, and later Phrates, son of King Phrates'. Horace finds a different formula. Phraates IV may have regained the throne through his popularity with the people of Parthia, but true kingly power is a matter of virtue, and Virtue grants kingship only to the man who (like Sallustius Crispus of course) can resist the temptations of wealth. The end of this ode, as analysed in a magisterial treatment by Lebek, is Stoic not only in the praise of the man who resists desire, but also in the favourite Stoic concept of the personification of Virtue, the Stoic insistence upon the *true* meaning of words, and the adaptation of the familiar Stoic paradox that only the wise man is king.

The Stoic elements in this ode have led scholars to read it as an expression of Stoic values, and since the message is often tooled to the man in this *ad hominem* poetry, they have concluded that Sallustius himself is likely to have shown an interest in Stoicism. The Stoic is being praised in Stoic terms. The difficulty about this theory is that it has no support from any evidence. Sallustius inherited from his great-uncle not only the Horti Sallustiani but also a huge fortune and a sumptuous house, and his obituary in Tacitus, *Annals* 3. 30. 2–3 suggests that he lived accordingly: 'Contrary to tradition, by reason of his refinement and sophistication, surrounded by abundance and affluence, he came close to living a life of self-indulgence. He had, however, a vigour of mind fit for great affairs, and all the sharper the more he gave an appearance of sleepiness and inactivity. He was, therefore, next to Maecenas in the confidence of the emperors while Maecenas lived, and after his death second to none.' This discrepancy can be explained by guessing, again without any evidence, that the young Sallustius had Stoic leanings in 23 BC when Horace was producing these odes, but had lapsed into a life of luxury before his death in AD 20.

There is another solution. If we guess rather that young Sallustius fully enjoyed the rich inheritance he received on the death of his great-uncle in 35 BC, it would be exceedingly likely that his good fortune and his enjoyment of it would have aroused some envy and some criticism, particularly when he was beginning to advance in the counsels of Augustus. There must have been some who grumbled to see Maecenas being succeeded as intimate adviser to Augustus by Sallustius Crispus, another omnicompetent hedonist (the stereotype is discussed in detail in Woodman's note on Velleius, 2. 88. 2). What better way could Horace have found of rebutting such criticism than by opposing it with arguments from Stoicism? This guess makes good sense of the first stanza and its insistence on the use, not the hoarding, of money. It also fits the central stanzas attacking acquisitiveness, which is a vice Sallustius would not have needed to practise because his wealth was inherited, not acquired. Besides, we may take it from the epigram by Crinagoras, who was in Rome in 25 BC when Horace was writing these odes, that Sallustius was a generous patron of literature. But this theory suits most closely the last two stanzas with their attack on popular opinion. These stanzas would immediately be understandable if Horace were arguing against some vulgar gossip attacking Sallustius. Part of Horace's defence is his insistence on the importance of calling things by their proper names, the implication being that what the malicious call extravagance is in truth the enlightened use of money, defensible even on Stoic terms. Sallustius can gaze at vast accumulations of wealth [and walk away] without a backward glance.

My insertion reveals a slight gap in Horace's logic. From the 'deliberately ambiguous opening maxim' as Nisbet and Hubbard call it, to the last line where 'at first sight Horace's phrase seems nonsensical' this ode has its share of tortuous, complex, and unlovely philosophical elements. This is why it has received a bad press. Commager (79) writes: 'Horace never raises the poem from the level of frigid ingenuity.' Quinn (199)

III

AEQUAM memento rebus in arduis
servare mentem, non secus si bonis
ab insolenti temperatam
laetitia, moriture Delli

seu maestus omni tempore vixeris,
seu te in remoto gramine per dies
festos reclinatum bearis
interiore nota Falerni.

quo pinus ingens albaque populus
umbram hospitalem consociare amant
ramis? quid obliquo laborat
lympha fugax trepidare rivo?

judges it 'a curiously unsatisfying poem'. Connor (166) finds 'a harshness of thought and language and imagery'. The interpretation here advanced would agree with these judgements and would take them as tributes to the poem. It is Horace's tactic to dare to speak in these austere tones in order to defend a patron of literature who lived like an Epicurean, in terms which would suggest that Sallustius would win the approval of the strictest Stoic.

Support for this interpretation may be found in the placing of the poem. In his opening programmatic statement at 2. 1. 37–40 Horace has just undertaken to write cheerful poems and love poems. He follows this undertaking immediately with this solemn, crabbed, and convoluted little sermon. We are in the hands of a manipulator, performing behind a screen, and his strategy includes variety and surprise. This suspicion hardens when we come to the wine and roses of the next ode, or when we think of the cameo which follows the great Cleopatra ode, 1. 37. Horace is writing poems, not expounding a creed. At all times we have to be wary of his philosophizing and remember what he will be saying to the world three years later, when he issues the first book of the *Epistles* (1. 1. 13–19), that he is irremediably inconsistent in his views, and that he has not sworn allegiance to any one school. We notice that Horace lays hold of whatever philosophy may suit his poem, and often makes fun of it.

III

Remember to keep your mind level when the path
is steep, and no less in good times to keep it tempered
   and well away from extravagant joy,
      Dellius, who will die

whether you spend every minute of your life in gloom,
or bless yourself lying all the long days of festivals
   in secluded meadows, drinking Falernian
      from the back of the cellar.

Why do the huge pine and the white poplar
love to ally their branches in hospitable shade?
   Why does the rushing river twist and strain
      as it scurries along?

huc vina et unguenta et nimium brevis
flores amoenae ferre iube rosae,
dum res et aetas et sororum
fila trium patiuntur atra.

cedes coemptis saltibus et domo
villaque flavus quam Tiberis lavit;
cedes, et exstructis in altum
divitiis potietur heres.

divesne prisco natus ab Inacho
nil interest an pauper et infima
de gente sub divo moreris,
victima nil miserantis Orci.

omnes eodem cogimur, omnium
versatur urna serius ocius
sors exitura et nos in aeternum
exsilium impositura cumbae.

'Give orders to bring wine here', *huc vina . . . ferre iube*' (line 13) tells us that Horace is asking Dellius to issue directions to his slaves for a symposium. Like 1. 11, 27, and 28 this is a dramatic monologue. If we are to understand it we have to be on the alert for clues to the dramatic setting and the character of speaker and listener.

Horace is talking to Dellius in the shade of a pine and a poplar by a winding, rushing river. He will have given a wave of the hand as he mentions the trees and another as he mentions the river. In the normal way of dramatic monologues lines 17–20 tell us that Dellius is rich and has bought up landed estates (*saltus* are wooded pastures, often in hilly country). He has also a house in Rome and a villa on the banks of the Tiber, where Horace is now suggesting that they should drink some wine together.

The poem urges a simple message, 'Enjoy life, for you will die', and everything fits this message except the advice in lines 2–4 not to be too elated in good times. Dellius had earned the title of the 'stunt rider of the Civil Wars', *desultorem bellorum civilium* (Seneca, *Suasoriae* 1. 7) for his conspicuous agility in changing allegiance from Caesar to Cassius to Antony and finally to Octavian before Actium. But in 23 BC that was all in the past and he is now a secure and substantial figure, worthy to be honoured alongside Pollio, Sallustius, and Proculeius in the opening odes of this second book. Horace may have judged that the simple hedonistic message, 'Enjoy life, for you will die' was a little slight for such a

Tell them to bring out the wine and fragrant oils
and all-too-short-lived flowers of the lovely rose,
while your age and means and the black threads
of the three sisters permit.

You will leave the upland woods and pastures you have bought,
your house in Rome, and villa lapped by the yellow Tiber,
you will leave them and your heir
will take possession of your high-built wealth.

It makes no difference whether you are rich and of the stock
of ancient Inachus, or a pauper born in the gutter
and living under the open sky—
you are the victim of Orcus, who knows no pity.

We are all herded to the same place. All our lots
are turning in the urn, and later or sooner
they will be shaken out and will put us
on the boat for an exile that never ends.

person, perhaps even needless, and at the risk of clouding his argument, has added dignity to it in the formal balance of the opening rhetoric. But even the warning not to take too much pleasure in prosperity is consistent with the teaching of Epicurus, as represented in his fragment 488 (Usener), 'The weak soul puffs itself up in easy times and is cast down in disasters.' There is another philosophical touch which helps to preserve the high-minded atmosphere. The symposium Horace proposes is no drunken rout, but a scene described in terms which evoke the ideal philosophical contentment of the Epicureans. True, the Lucretian passage refers to the simple pleasures of the poor and not a symposium on a rich man's estate, but it is surely in Horace's mind at this point:

> cum tamen inter se prostrati in gramine molli
> propter aquae rivum sub ramis arboris altae
> non magnis opibus iucunde corpora curant,
> praesertim cum tempestas adridet et anni
> tempora conspergunt viridantis floribus herbas.
>
> (Lucretius, 2. 29–33)

> but when they lie together in soft grass
> near a stream of water under the branches of a tall tree
> and enjoy themselves at no great expense,
> particularly when the weather smiles and the season
> of the year sprinkles the green of the grass with flowers.

Like Shakespeare in *Hamlet*, Horace sometimes seems to write in tags. What makes the opening of this ode so memorable may partly be the sculptured expressiveness of the Latin, whereby *aequam* is joined by the great arch of the hyperbaton to *mentem*, and the music of those two words enjoining calmness of mind is enhanced by *memento* and set off by the contrasting music of adversity in *rebus in arduis*. But the force of the maxim is not yet exhausted. Here, as so often, Horace shows us a glimpse of a metaphor. There is no need to see it in this way but, granted that the *level* is in active contrast with the *steep*, when Dellius then hears that in good times he should keep his mind restrained, checked (the same verb *temperare* is used of controlling a horse in 1. 8. 7), we are offered a glance of a rider holding back his mount on a steep slope. The stanza then ends with a cruel shock. Instead of some complimentary adjective, the term applied to Dellius is *moriture*, 'Dellius, about to die'.

In the first line of the next stanza there is a twinge of amusement at the thought that anyone could spend *all* their time in misery. The alternative is then described in loving detail. The meadow is secluded in the sense that it is far from crowds and the demands of business or politics. The whole long day is devoted to an *al fresco* symposium and the participants bless themselves, where *te . . . bearis* lightly hints that their great enjoyment has divine approval. Finally in this stanza, the wine is superb and of an old vintage, kept at the back of the rack in the cellar. Delicious. This last word is not flippancy, but an attempt to draw attention to the fact that poetry can please not only because of its imagery, sound, language, thought, and other features that can be talked about, but simply because what it refers to is pleasant.

This is certainly part of the beauty of the next stanza. But the tone changes with the teasing rhetorical questions as Horace asks for what purpose trees and water behave as they do. Horace knows as well as we do, that trees and streams do not have purposes. The huge pine and the white poplar are an example of a poetic figure which has been called the *schema Horatianum* (see Schmidt). A clear example of this schema occurs at 3. 13. 6–7, where Horace writes that red blood stains the cold water of a fountain and so suggests that the blood is warm and the water is clear. So here the huge pine is dark and the white poplar is slender. This is confirmed if, as seems likely, Horace refers to the stone or umbrella pine, which is common in Italy from Ravenna southwards. This *pinus pinea* rises to 75 feet with '*broad dark dome* from short bole' according to Mitchell (190). The white poplar, the foliage of whose crown is 'strikingly white' (Mitchell, 181) is certainly a slender tree. These two trees literally 'love to ally a hospitable shade with their branches'. The words *amant*, *hospitalem*, and *consociare* certainly personify the trees and suggest that they are engaged in some sort of affectionate contact. All these standard items of popular philosophy are here charged with suggestion. As Dellius, for instance, is invited to be at leisure, the labour of the river, described by the typical Alcaic effect (see Index of Topics) in the long syllables of the third line of the stanza, is followed by swiftly flying anxiety in the short syllables of the fourth, and all this is somehow related to the endless haste and anxiety of city life. Horace, of course, does not put this forward as a formal analogy. The description and the Alcaic effect are more like a harmonic to the music of the verse. Different ears hear different harmonics.

The notion that poetry can please because what it refers to is pleasing receives striking confirmation in lines 13–14. Wine, perfumed oils for the hair, and rose blooms were all pleasing to Romans in themselves and because they were associated with delightful symposia. Horace often appeals to the senses not by sensuous descriptions of experiences, but simply by mentioning them. So wine is not only delicious to the eye, the nose, and the palate but is also the stimulus for all manner of delightful conversation. Unguents appeal to the nose and also to the Roman's memory of sleek hair shining on beautiful heads. Roses appeal to the eyes and the nose, and even more to memories of petals floating in bowls of wine and blooms wilting in garlands by the end of the evening to remind drinkers how short life is, and how much shorter is beauty. There is no cleverness or sensuousness in the wording of the first eight Latin words in this stanza, but they are rich in sensuous and emotional power because they mention three delightful things, and the poetry is all the richer because the three pleasures are followed by three human limitations. The thought glides from the all-too-short-lived blooms of the lovely rose to the circumstances of Dellius' life, to age, and to the three sisters who cut the threads of our lives.

These circumstances are the subject of the next stanza. Dellius is told that he will leave his home in Rome and his villa laved by the yellow Tiber. The very ordinariness of the adjective is part of the strength of the writing. Dellius knew the scene well. He would look out over his familiar view and reflect that he would have to leave it, while his heir would take possession of his high-built wealth. In 2. 2. 24 the wealth was heaped up, but here the context points rather to building than to heaping. Perhaps Dellius had a tower or towers in one of his houses, as Maecenas had on the Esquiline, and Sestius at Cosa (3. 29. 10 and 1. 4. 14).

All this is the material ambience of an affluent society. As the ode ends, the vision is universalized to include the poor, and opens to mythology in Inachus, the legendary first king of Argos, Orcus, the king of the Underworld, and Charon, the ferryman of the River Styx. But here too, in the dark of the Underworld, there is a glimmer of a metaphor. In line 24 Dellius is told that for all his wealth and perhaps ancestry, he will become a victim of Orcus. A sacrifice in Rome might have been an animal, a pig, a sheep, or an ox, and it would have been driven to sacrifice by the temple attendants. In line 25, as in 1. 10. 17–20 and 1. 24. 18, it is human beings who are driven to the same place, herded like helpless animals. A different image follows in 25–6 where the urn full of lots is turned in hands we know not whose, and later or sooner every lot will leap out. With an uneasy movement we now come to a third image in this stanza. The lot coming out of the jar will put us on board a boat, and the whole strange double image is linked in sound by *versatur urna*, *sors exitura*, and *impositura*. Here too the Alcaic effect is heard and the great weight of the third line of the Alcaic becomes even more crippling by reason of the triple elision of *exitur*(*a*) before *et*, *aetern*(*um*) before *exsilium* in the next line, and *exsili*(*um*) before *impositura*, an accumulation unparalleled in the odes. Horace is now talking to all of us. Charon's boat will take us all into an exile from which there is no hope of recall. We know from the late poetry of Ovid how heartbreaking exile could be for a Roman, and a crucial part of the suffering was the loss of the way of life alluded to in lines 17–20.

This note began by asking how the character of Dellius is related to the poem. This enquiry should be taken further. According to the historians the younger Dellius was flexible, worldly, and unscrupulous. In the early 40s BC he served under Caesar's admiral Dolabella. After Caesar's assassination in 44 BC he changed sides and served under Cassius the conspirator and even offered to murder Dolabella. By 41 BC he had changed sides again and joined Antony, coaching Cleopatra in the arts of seduction and then in Alexandria teasing her about Egyptian wines as compared with Falernian (see line 8 of this ode), writing her lascivious letters, pimping, and perhaps doing even more for Antony afterwards (details, as ever, in Nisbet and Hubbard). Much of this is little more than gossip, and after this, in the 20s, we know nothing about Dellius except what we deduce from this ode, that he was accepted by Augustus (confirmed by Seneca, *De Clementia* 1. 10. 1), and that he was wealthy. The danger of interpreting the ode in the light of Dellius' known character is that our knowledge is out of date. We do not know how he was behaving in the

20s BC, and even if it were plausible that Horace is pressing the middle way upon a vacillating or calculating temperament, or ingratiatingly recommending hedonism to a confirmed hedonist, none of these conjectures gives much point to the poem.

It may be more helpful to imagine that it was written to comfort and cheer Dellius for some sadness in his life, perhaps an illness, perhaps bereavement. If we guess, and of course it is only a guess, that Dellius in his late fifties was suffering in some such way (Horace's first readers would have known about it), the first line of the poem has a much sharper application, and the whole ode suddenly takes on a different dimension. It compliments him on his past equanimity in happy times and urges him to show a similar self-control in his present suffering. If he is ill or is mourning the death of someone he loved, the astonishing vocative *moriture* becomes even bolder than we realized, reminding him that he too must die. The word *maestus* in line 5 is frequently used of mourning, as in Horace, *Satires* 1. 2. 3 where lovers of the theatre are mourning the death of Tigellius, *maestum . . . morte Tigelli*, and the last stanza takes on new meaning, 'we must all die, not only the deceased whom you loved, but also yourself who mourn and I who offer consolation'. It will be objected that on this interpretation, the consolation offered in this ode is tactless or even brutal, but we have seen in 1. 24 that Horace does not go in for easy comfort.

The opening three odes of this second book make an apparently incoherent group. The passionate evocation of the Civil Wars as seen in Pollio's *Historiae* ends at 1. 37–40 with Horace announcing that he is going to write cheerful poems and love poems, such as suit a lighter plectrum, *leviore plectro*. This lighter plectrum then proceeds to strum a crabbed Stoic sermon, and that is now followed by an Epicurean poem of which more than half is devoted to death. At the end of the note on *Odes* 2. 2 I suggested that Horace was by implication demonstrating his own fickleness and his own independence of mind. There may be more to it than that. A close comparison of the second and third odes shows that they have many details in common. I note *temperato* and *temperatam* in the third line of each poem and the striking syntax, unparalleled in Horace, whereby long conditional clauses are attached to adjectives in the vocative case: compare *inimice nisi* with *moriture seu*. There are other verbal resemblances but even more important is the doctrinal correspondence. In the 'Stoic' ode Sallustius is praised for using wealth rather than hoarding it. In the 'Epicurean' ode Dellius is urged to enjoy his wealth. Modern scholars tend to take Horace's philosophy seriously. This is a mistake he does not make. It would be well within the scope of this elusive writer to be gently mocking philosophical technicalities and bigotry, hinting at the disagreements of the schools, and for comparison laying out his own simple and obvious way of thinking. Philosophers and religious persons tend to disapprove: 'Take thine ease, eat, drink, and be

---

IV

Ne sit ancillae tibi amor pudori,
Xanthia Phoceu, prius insolentem
serva Briseis niveo colore
  movit Achillem;

movit Aiacem Telamone natum
forma captivae dominum Tecmessae;
arsit Atrides medio in triumpho
  virgine rapta,

barbarae postquam cecidere turmae
Thessalo victore et ademptus Hector
tradidit fessis leviora tolli
  Pergama Grais.

nescias an te generum beati
Phyllidis flavae decorent parentes:
regium certe genus et penatis
  maeret iniquos.

crede non illam tibi de scelesta
plebe delectam, neque sic fidelem,
sic lucro aversam potuisse nasci
  matre pudenda.

bracchia et vultum teretesque suras
integer laudo; fuge suspicari
cuius octavum trepidavit aetas
  claudere lustrum.

merry' says the rich man to his soul at Luke 12: 19, and God replies 'Thou fool'. But there is still poetic power in Horace's nexus of life and death, of love and the loss of love, of wine, flowers, and the passing of time.

IV

There is no need, Phocian Xanthias, to be ashamed
of your love for a slave girl. Ere now the slave Briseis
with her white skin moved the heart
  of proud Achilles;

the beauty of the captive Tecmessa moved her master,
Ajax, son of Telamon; the son of Atreus in his hour
of triumph burned with love
  for the maid who was ravished

after the barbarian squadrons had fallen
to the Thessalian victor, and the removal
of Hector made it a lighter task for weary Greeks
  to raze Troy to the ground.

For all you know your flaxen-haired Phyllis
has wealthy parents, a credit to any son-in-law.
The family, no doubt of it, is royal and mourns
  the gods who have turned against it.

Do not imagine that you could have picked such a one
out of the gutter, or that one so faithful,
so unmercenary, could have a mother
  to be ashamed of.

I praise her arms, her face, her shapely calves—
but am immune. Do not for a moment
suspect a man when Time has raced
  to close his fourth decade.

Odes 2.4

Be not deterred by the pompous tone of the opening. This is parody. At the end of the first ode in this book Horace tells us that he will be using a lighter plectrum to compose cheerful poems and love poems. After cheating our expectations in the next two odes, at last he writes a cheerful love poem, adopting his familiar posture as the Professor of Love, *Praeceptor Amoris* (compare 1. 8, 27, 29) to tease a young man for being in love with a slave girl. According to Pliny, *Letters* 2. 20. 9 the *Lex Scholastica* rules that exempla should be adduced in threes. Here Horace provides three exempla.

In the first half of the poem the teasing consists mainly of epic parody using three linguistic devices characteristic of Greek and Latin epic. First, stock epithets are conspicuous in Homer, as when Achilles is called swift-footed, *podas okus*. Here he is 'arrogant', *insolentem* and Briseis is literally 'with snow-white colour', the latter a hint at the compound adjectives favoured by Homer, like white-armed, *leukolenos*. Even 'Phocian Xanthias' in the first line is claiming some such epic resonance for this slight character. A second epic feature is the patronymic, as in the first line of the *Iliad*, 'Sing to me, O Goddess, of Achilles, son of Peleus'. So in this ode in line 6 Ajax is the son of Telamon, and later in line 6 we are not even given the name. *Atrides* is enough to identify Agamemnon. This, in turn, is an example of the third epic device, antonomasia, whereby a person is referred to obliquely without the use of a name, as in the eighth line of *Paradise Lost* where Moses is called 'That Shepherd who first taught the chosen Seed'. This trick pleases readers by setting them problems they can solve as they go, and by reminding them of familiar stories. Milton's readers are also nudged into realizing that the shepherd Moses, visited by the *Heav'nly* Muse while tending his sheep 'on the secret *top* of Oreb or of Sinai', is a sounder authority than the shepherd Hesiod, taught by the *Heliconian* Muses as he tended his lambs *under* the holy mountain of Helicon in his *Theogony* 22–3. There are other examples of antonomasia in this ode. Cassandra the prophetess, daughter of King Priam, is called the ravished maid, the Trojans are barbarian squadrons, and Achilles the Thessalian victor.

There is more fun with epic in the application of heroic exempla to this unheroic situation. Briseis moved Achilles, but that is more than Odysseus, Phoinix, and Ajax could do on their embassy unforgettably described in the ninth book of the *Iliad*. Tecmessa moved Ajax and that is more than the horse-taming Trojans and their allies could do for all their striving as he stood immovable like a mule in a cornfield in *Iliad* 11. 558–65. The language of these two exempla is beautifully tooled, with the heroes as the objects of the verbs *Briseis . . . movit Achillem*, *movit Aiacem . . . forma Tecmessae*. The third example rises to a climax as Agamemnon becomes the active subject of his verb. Captive women moved Achilles and Ajax, but Agamemnon burned, *arsit Atrides*. He burned in his hour of triumph and this is also part of the climax. He caught fire according to Horace at the famous burning of the city, a conceit boiled down from the other great serious metaphorist in Latin poetry:

> numquam Tyndaridis formae *conflatus* amore
> *ignis* Alexandri Phrygio sub pectore *gliscens*
> *clara accendisset* saevi certamina belli,
> nec clam durateus Troianis Pergama partu
> *inflammasset* equos nocturno Graiugenarum.
>
> (Lucretius, 1. 473–7)

> Never would the *fire* which love for the beauty of the daughter
> of Tyndareus *blew* to a blaze in the breast of Paris have *spread*
> to *light* the *bright* struggles of pitiless war, nor would the oaken horse
> with its unseen, night-time issue of the sons of the Greeks
> have *put to flame* the citadel of the Trojans.

This, of course, is sublime poetry, not a melody for Horace's lighter plectrum, but in this epic parody Lucretius exploits two of the techniques we have just met in Horace. The daughter of Tyndareus is Helen, by antonomasia and matronymic, and Lucretius, for his own sardonic purposes, puts the patronymic through strange paces to make an oaken horse the mother of the sons of Greeks, *Graiugenarum*, particularly since this mother was made of oak, *dourateus*, a Greek word which occurs only here in surviving Latin. But the essence of this high poetry is Pindaric rather than epic, namely the sustained metaphor as noted in the words associated with fire italicized in the Lucretius above, surrounding the totally different metaphor of childbirth, and culminating in a thundering four-word line (477). In Horace's ode also there is immediately a different metaphor. After the Trojan squadrons fell, *cecidere*, the removal of Hector, *ademptus Hector*, handed over the citadel of Troy, now lighter to be lifted, *leviora tolli*, which also means 'easier to be destroyed'.

Another typical Horatian feature in these first stanzas is the juxtaposition of opposites (see West 1973). It was a slave, *serva*, who moved arrogant Achilles, *insolentem serva*, and the beauty of a captive which moved her master Ajax, *captivae dominum*, but Agamemnon blazed up with love for a ravished virgin, *virgine rapta*. Sometimes this is tamely translated as 'the virgin dragged off into captivity'. But surely the force of a word depends upon its neighbours. We do not need to look at section 8 of the *Oxford Latin Dictionary* under *rapere* to know what a *virgo rapta* is. The vivid version of the story here followed is that after the Trojan forces were defeated, Ajax Oileus raped Cassandra in the temple of Athena and that Agamemnon subsequently fell in love with her and took her back with him to Greece. Another juxtaposition comes at the climax of these stanzas of mock-heroic writing with *Pergama Grais*, where the citadel of Troy is destroyed by the Greeks. This third stanza is one long adverbial clause and Nisbet and Hubbard suggest that 'the trailing temporal clause is a mannerism of high poetry'.

The rising graph of these three stanzas leads into the ironic climax of lines 13–16, where the Homeric heroes are used as analogies for the love affair of Xanthias and Phyllis. Here *illam tibi* is the subtlest of all the juxtaposed opposites. Literally the clause means 'Believe her not to be chosen by you from the base common people' (and *de scelesta plebe* is a very strong expression), but any such version totally fails to convey the thrust of *crede non illam tibi*, 'Believe not her by you', implying 'Do not imagine that one such as she could have been chosen by one such as you from the gutter.'

The shapely calves of the last stanza have been felt to be risqué, and that is surely part of the humour. In this epic context the phrase is a glancing reminder of the Homeric compound adjective *kallisphuros*, 'of the beautiful ankles'. Horace has raised his eyes a little from *sphura*, the ankle, to *sura*, the calf. But he is not guilty of any grave impropriety. Although a matron's dress came down to her ankles, a maidservant's would be much shorter, a detail used by Horace himself in *Satires* 1. 2. 28–9. Phyllis is obviously a slave. Besides, as the *Praeceptor Amoris* explains, men in their forties are not interested in such things. The best comment on the word *teres*, 'shapely, exquisitely', is Munro's note on

---

V

NONDUM subacta ferre iugum valet
cervice, nondum munia comparis
aequare nec tauri ruentis
in Venerem tolerare pondus.

Lucretius, 1. 35, where the word is used to describe Venus' neck. Munro proves that it means 'of the proper shape, neither too thick or too thin. Thus a *teres cervix* is a neck that has the true outline of beauty, neither lean nor fleshy, neither too long or too short.'

A serious question has been raised. Who was Xanthias and where is the above drama unfolding? Xanthias is a Greek slave name, famously attached to the rascal who goes down to the Underworld with Dionysus in the *Frogs* of Aristophanes. But it makes nonsense of the poem to think of this Xanthias as a slave. The clue is in 1. 8, a poem similar in tone to this one. There the lover is given the Greek name Sybaris, but he had been engaged in the full military training programme of a young Roman in the Campus Martius. Whether he ever was a real character or not, he is clearly meant to be thought of as a Roman. This is normal Horatian practice. Perhaps he took this decision in order to lend the cachet of Greek to this Roman recreation of Greek lyric poetry. And Xanthias Phoceus perhaps sounded better in such contexts than, say, Sallustius Crispus or Gaius Proculeius. This brings out the humour of line 14, with its alarming suggestion that Xanthias is in danger of acquiring parents-in-law who were slaves.

This ode is written in the Sapphic stanza, which ends with a short line, the Adonius, and this metrical figure sometimes supports the sense. In line 4 the Adonius astonishes; in line 8 it is poignant; in line 12, a climactic juxtaposition of opposites. In the remaining stanzas the last lines are on a rising scale of pseudo-poignancy, till the greatest lie of all in line 24. To confirm this 'Sapphic effect' we could look back to the second ode in this book, where the first stanza rises to a condensed climax in line 4; shrinks from the vast to the minute in line 12; falls away with a whimper in line 16; rushes to join two stanzas at line 20; and denies a backward glance in 24. These attempts to express the Sapphic effect are of course failures. Music cannot be paraphrased. But it pays to listen.

V

She's not broken in yet and her neck hasn't the strength
to bear the yoke. She can't share duties
  with a partner yet or bear the weight
    of a bull plunging into love.

circa virentis est animus tuae
campos iuvencae, nunc fluviis gravem
solantis aestum, nunc in udo
ludere cum vitulis salicto

praegestientis. tolle cupidinem
immitis uvae: iam tibi lividos
distinguet Autumnus racemos
purpureo varius colore.

iam te sequetur: currit enim ferox
aetas et illi quos tibi dempserit
apponet annos; iam proterva
fronte petet Lalage maritum,

dilecta quantum non Pholoe fugax,
non Chloris albo sic umero nitens
ut pura nocturno renidet
luna mari, Cnidiusve Gyges,

quem si puellarum insereres choro,
mire sagaces falleret hospites
discrimen obscurum solutis
crinibus ambiguoque vultu.

This poem owes a great deal to Anacreon, fragment 417:

> Why look at me out of the corner of your eyes, you Thracian filly,
> and run away without a sign of pity? You seem to think
> I'm an ignorant fool. But let me tell you,
> I could nicely slip the bit in and take the reins in hand
> to steer you round the turning-posts of the course.
> But now you graze the meadows, playing and cavorting
> for want of a skilled rider who knows about horses.

Beside the Horace the Anacreon is light and elegant. Perhaps part of its lightness comes from the delicacy of the details, none of which gives a clear sexual indication until the very last word of the Greek, *epembaten*, rider. The features of the filly's life are chosen primarily for their own sake, for delight, not as vehicles of sexual *double-entendre*. By contrast Horace's ode is often condemned for its tastelessness or brutality, with particular reference to the weight of the plunging bull.

This is an injustice. The two poems are entirely different in their *mise-en-scène*. Anacreon is flirting with a young girl, amusing her, tempting

Odes 2.5

That young heifer of yours still has her mind
on grassy meadows, finding relief
  from oppressive heat in rivers, or longing
    to begin playing with bull calves

in willow marshes. Banish your desire
for the unripe grape. Autumn in all his variety
  will soon mark out the blue clusters for you,
    tinging them with purple.

She'll soon be following you. Time runs
on untamed and will credit her with the years
  it takes from you. Lalage will soon be butting
    her mate with lusty forehead

and be loved more than the elusive Pholoe,
more than Chloris, whose white shoulder gleams
  like the pure moon glinting
    on the night sea, more than Gyges.

Put him in a dance with girls and the subtle difference
would wonderfully deceive your most perceptive guests—
  that flowing hair
    and that ambiguous face.

her, careful not to frighten her. The poem is an attempt to catch the tones of seduction in poetry. Horace, on the other hand, is urging a man *not* to seduce a girl. The picture of the bull crashing down on the delicate little calf is not tasteless brutality, but an appeal to the better nature of the would-be seducer, a realization of what lovemaking would be to a girl of that age. The event is seen from the point of view of the girl. Focalization.

But Horace is condemned also for the grossness of other details in his account of the life of the heifer. Scholars have been indefatigable in finding sexual overtones: at *munia* in line 2, where the heifer cannot equal the duties of a yoke-mate, they confidently see conjugal duties; at 6–8, where meadows are taken to hint at virginity *and* at erotic activities, where the cold water is held to have antaphrodisiac properties, where the heat, *aestum*, seems to hint at feverish emotions. The willow swamp is then deemed a suitable place for conducting a love affair and the colour of the grape recalls the veins on a woman's breast. The neck in the first line of the poem is even held to plunge into gynaecology and signify the *cervix vulvae*. It is absurd to press all these metaphorical details into sexual service. Like Anacreon, Horace is taking delight in his metaphor and enjoying its details for their own sake. The movement of the poem is destroyed if the dictionaries are scoured to prove that every word is a *double entendre*. This is pansemanticism run riot (see West 1995*a*: 160–1). A simple proof of this ought to be found where the grape becomes purple when it ripens. Turning purple is not one of the anxieties of pubescent girls.

Take for instance the opening of Horace's poem. Here too the details of the metaphor should be enjoyed for themselves, not milked for their sexual application. The first statement about the heifer is even more precise in the Latin than in translation. Strictly it is the neck which is not 'broken in', literally 'subdued', and the heifer which does not have the strength to bear the yoke. Even if she had, she could not pull equally with a yoke-fellow, which the Romans knew would be agony for oxen and driver (see *Odes* 1. 33. 10–12 and Plautus, *Aulularia* 228–30). Romans would also have known that unbroken heifers would be left to graze and build up their strength and that cattle try to keep cool in hot weather by standing in rivers. The climax comes at *praegestientis*, and here at last the sexual allusion surfaces. The verb *gestire* implies impatient longing, as in the first citation in the *Oxford Latin Dictionary* from Plautus, *Casina* 471, where the old man is desperate to kiss his bailiff's bride, *iam osculari gestio*. The prefix *prae* in line 9 of this ode means that the heifer is longing *in advance*, precociously, to play with the bullocks, but she has not yet dared to do so. Perhaps in rereading, we may find a hint of conjugal duties in the *munia*, the duties in the first line, but it is just a light hint, like the turning-posts in the racecourse in the Anacreon.

Another striking difference between the poems is the astonishing switch of metaphor in line 9. Without warning the incipient sexual stirrings of the heifer are followed by the command, in pseudo-lofty language, 'Banish your desire for the unripe grape'. This is so pointed in the Latin that it must be designed as a deliberate effect. We have already noticed three different metaphors sweeping past in quick succession at 2. 3. 25–8, the herding, the shaking of the urn, the boat that takes us into exile. At 2. 4. 9–12 we have seen a metaphor eked out by puns, where the removal of Hector makes it lighter for the weary Greeks to raise Troy and the punning meaning is that it makes it easier for them to raze Troy to the ground. Now in 2. 5 we have this violent juxtaposition of two entirely different metaphors, and more to come. Conte (1994: 311), following the early Nisbet and Hubbard (1970: p. xxii), refers to Horace's 'cautious employment of metaphors'. For cautious, read daring. On 2. 4. 9–12

Martindale (5) speaks of 'discontinuous imagery' and suggests that Callimachus may be the model. Perhaps Pindar is nearer:

> Steer your people with a just rudder
> and forge your tongue on an anvil that is not false.
> If any spark of meanness flies off,
> coming from you it is held to be great.
> You are the steward of plenty.
>
> (Pindar, *Pythian* 1. 86–8)

It is easy to read the Horatian passage as a strange and awkward turn, but there is no doubt that it is intended. It is as though he is testing how far he can go to bring into this lightweight poem the audacity and freedom of Pindar's choral odes.

In the grape metaphor which follows, once again the natural details are vividly described. Autumn, personified, is *varius*, because of the increased colour-range of his season, and the word order presents it to our eyes and ears by putting Autumn himself between the grape clusters, *racemos*, and their epithet, *lividos*, and placing his adjective *varius* between *purpureo* and *colore*. Much of the expressiveness of Latin poetic language comes from the flexibility of its word order, in particular the separation of words which belong together, hyperbaton. It is this freedom which makes possible the interlacing of adjectives and nouns in this stanza and gives force as we read to this evocation of the abundance and variety of autumn.

The poem now takes another sharp turn. When Horace says 'She will soon be following you', we may detect an imitation of one of the most famous lines in the whole of ancient love poetry, Sappho, 1. 21, 'for even if she's running away, she'll soon be pursuing'. We suspect that Horace, who tends to make fun of Sappho (see West 1995*a* on 1. 13. 1–8, 22. 21–2, and 2. 13. 24–6), is applying it to a young cow and a bull, and the suspicion will be confirmed when Lalage starts butting her mate in line 15. But first Horace moves to a new metaphor, 'Time untamed [*ferox*, "fierce"] is running and will put to her account the years it will take away from you.' The consolation we expect would be that in twelve months the girl will be a year older. If any comparison were to be made, we would expect to hear that they will each be older, but the year will make more difference to the girl than to the mature man. That is strikingly not what Horace says. On the face of it what he does say is false, 'Time will give her the years it takes away from you', thus making you younger. We cannot entertain this nonsense and are therefore driven to the only possible sense, that every year added to the girl's tally will take a year away from the tally of years that the man *will* live. Such a reminder of age and death seems wholly out of place in this argument and in this cheerful poem. Horace cannot be arguing 'be patient: a year from now you will be a year nearer death'. The startling discontinuous imagery in line 9 seemed to be an experiment in the Pindaric style. If that suggestion has any force, it may be that the experiment continues with this portentous and obscure moralization, not unlike many such utterances in the odes of Pindar. Such a turn would perhaps help to characterize the speaker. Horace is talking as the counsellor, the *Praeceptor Amoris*, and lending weight, or pretending to lend weight, to his counsel by the portentous gravity with which he expounds it.

This poem is a sequence of threes. The first tricolon fills the first stanza, the second stanza is nearly another, and the last two stanzas list three previous lovers of the addressee. In the middle of this sequence we are pressed to hear the tricolon in *iam distinguet*, *iam sequetur*, *iam petet*, 'soon Autumn will mark out, soon she will follow, soon Lalage will butt'. The rhetoric of the poem therefore makes it difficult to defend the present tense, *petit*, which occurs in some of the manuscripts.

In the last stanza we move into a different world. 'The romantic and evocative descriptions . . . The symmetry of the love affairs, and their sexual indifference, evoke the artificial, amoral world of Hellenistic poetry' argue Nisbet and Hubbard (1978: 79), and they refer to Theocritus, 2. 44–5; Callimachus, *Epigram* 25; and Virgil, *Eclogues* 10. 37. The learned etymological play with the names of the lovers adds to that impression. We met harsh Pholoe as a hard-hearted girl in 1. 33 and noted that Pholoe was also the name of a mountain known for its rugged rocks. Chloris means pale as well as green and Pausanias, 2. 21. 10 tells us that Chloris, the one surviving daughter of Niobe, was rendered pale for life by seeing the killing of all her brothers and sisters. Gyges was the great king of Lydia, a country famous for its luxury and sexual voluptuousness, and Cnidos was the shrine of Aphrodite.

This poem started as though it was to be an adaptation of fragment 417 of Anacreon. Some of Horace's odes begin with a 'motto', a line which is a translation of the first line of some early Greek lyric, and which is followed by Horace's own departure from that base, as though he were saying 'We know the Greek poem. Now let's hear where Latin can go from that same starting-point'. In this 'motto poem' the departure is radical, changing the *mise-en-scène*, the *dramatis personae*, the imagery, and the tone and producing something totally new. The discontinuous imagery in the first three stanzas and the moralizing generalization in the fourth suggest the manner of Pindar. There is even a link with Philodemus (*Palatine Anthology* 5. 124. 1–2), the Greek philosopher and poet, a close associate of Horace's friend Virgil, who wrote of Lysidice whose 'grape cluster is not yet darkening as it puts on its first maidenly grace'. We then hear Horace saying 'she will soon be following you' and see that he has transposed Sappho's famous prophecy from human beings to livestock. The last two stanzas move to the Hellenistic world. It is as though this is an experimental poem in which Horace is trying to stretch the mould of Latin lyric which he himself has created. Perhaps it is part of his grand intention, as announced in *Odes* 1. 1, to join the canon of the great lyric poets of Greece by combining the resources of the choral odes of Pindar and the monodic lyric of Alcaeus, Anacreon, and Sappho, including even a whiff of Hellenistic epigram at the end of the poem. Horace speaks with many voices and yet always speaks with his own.

Many scholars believe that in this poem he is addressing himself, as Catullus does in *Poems* 8, lamenting his infatuation with a woman who does not love him: 'Poor Catullus, stop playing the fool', *Miser Catulle, desinas ineptire*. This is unlikely. In the Catullus poem we know from the first two words that the poet is speaking to himself, whereas there is no such guidance at all in the Horace. True, Catullus has a line which is very like line 17 of the Horace, where he says that Lesbia was loved as no other woman will ever be loved, *amata nobis quantum amabitur nulla*, but the poems differ totally in tone. Catullus, 8 purports to be an anguished introspection and carefully simulates a muddled stream of consciousness. Horace on the other hand is cool, detached, sophisticated, ironic. This is not the anguished lover in unhappy soliloquy, but our old friend the *Praeceptor Amoris* counselling patience to a lover in a hurry, a policy which is wise, humorous, and exactly in line with Horace's posture in other poems.

VI

Septimi, Gadis aditure mecum et
Cantabrum indoctum iuga ferre nostra et
barbaras Syrtis, ubi Maura semper
  aestuat unda,

Tibur Argeo positum colono
sit meae sedes utinam senectae,
sit modus lasso maris et viarum
  militiaeque!

unde si Parcae prohibent iniquae,
dulce pellitis ovibus Galaesi
flumen et regnata petam Laconi
  rura Phalantho.

ille terrarum mihi praeter omnis
angulus ridet, ubi non Hymetto
mella decedunt viridique certat
  baca Venafro,

ver ubi longum tepidasque praebet
Iuppiter brumas, et amicus Aulon
fertili Baccho minimum Falernis
  invidet uvis.

ille te mecum locus et beatae
postulant arces; ibi tu calentem
debita sparges lacrima favillam
  vatis amici.

Gades (Cadiz) is at the ends of the earth in the south-west corner of Spain beyond the pillars of Hercules. The Cantabrians in north Spain had always resisted the Romans. Augustus himself fought bitter campaigns against them in 26–25 BC, but they were not finally subdued until 20 BC by Agrippa. The Syrtes are the sandbanks on the Libyan coast, scene of the fearful storm of sand and sea at the beginning of Virgil's *Aeneid*, which was being written when his friend Horace produced these odes in 23 BC. Septimius would think nothing of going with his friend to any or all of those remote places, but this is a feint. Horace has something less arduous in mind.

VI

You who would go with me to Gades, Septimius, and
to the Cantabrian, who has never learned to bear our yoke, and
to the barbarian Syrtes, where the Moorish ocean
   forever boils,

let Tibur, founded by the settler from Argos,
be the resting place of my old age. Weary as I am,
let that be for me the end of roads and sea
   and soldiering.

But if the cruel Fates keep me from Tibur,
I shall make for the sweet waters of Galaesus
with its leather-coated sheep, and the country kingdom
   once ruled by Laconian Phalanthus.

This, above all others, is the corner of the earth
that smiles for me, where the honey does not yield
to Hymettus and the olive is a match
   for green Venafrum,

where Jupiter gives a long spring and warm winters,
where the Aulon valley is a friend
to fertile Bacchus and envies not at all
   the grapes of Falernum.

This is the place that calls out to you and me.
These are our blest citadels. There you will sprinkle
the tear you owe on the warm ashes
   of your friend the bard.

Tibur is the wealthy and spectacularly beautiful resort up in the hills 15 miles east of Rome, not violent like Spain or barbarous like North Africa, but founded by Tiburnus from Argos, a farmer-settler, *colonus*, suggesting Greek civilization and rural peace. Horace sums up in lines 7–8. He is tired of travel by sea and land and wants no more to do with war. Those who know him will think of his voyages to Athens to complete his education; the voyage back on which he suggests in *Odes* 3. 4. 28 that he was nearly drowned off Cape Palinurus; the rigours of the journey to Brundisium of *Satires* 1. 5 (but he must have taken many like it); and his traumatic involvement in the battle of Philippi, about which we shall hear in the next ode.

Failing Tibur, his second choice would be Tarentum, a colony of Sparta founded according to tradition by the Laconian Phalanthus in 708 BC (Laconia is the south-east area of the Peloponnese, governed by Sparta). Instead of the ever-seething ocean, he would have the Galaesus, a river sheep can drink from and find sweet (*gala* is the Greek for milk), and these are no ordinary sheep. Their wool was so precious that they wore leather coats to protect it. Herodotus gives an example of similar care in wool production in antiquity at 3. 113. 1–2, where he tells us that some Arabian sheep had such long tails that they were supported on wheeled trolleys. If any scepticism remains, it may be countered by the note in How and Wells's commentary, referring to the *ovis steatopyga* of Pallas in Asiatic Russia: 'Its tail is said in some cases to weigh over 70 lbs.; it is still at times protected by wheeled boards. (Woods, *Natural History*)'. Again, instead of violence Horace looks for a settled countryside; instead of barbarism, one of the ancient Greek foundations in south Italy, which was known as Magna Graecia, and one with honey as good as the fabled honey of Hymettus, the hill of Athens, olives as good as those from Venafrum in central Italy, and wine from the sheltered vineyards of Aulon (*aulon* is the Greek for a glen) as good as Falernian, one of the best of the Italian wines.

In the last stanza there is another surprise, where Horace contemplates his death. A Roman funeral pyre would be extinguished by sprinkling the glowing embers with wine or water. Septimius will pay his debt of friendship to Horace with a tear, one tear—Horace does not want a great display. It will fall on the ashes when they are warm, an experience vivid to the emotions of a Roman and vivid to the senses (Segal, 238, imagines it hissing), and all the more because it is referred to without any descriptive flourish or emotive language. The last two words in the Latin, *vatis amici*, are almost an epitaph: 'I am the great Augustan priest-prophet-poet, but I am also your friend.' Without being explicit, Horace has economically and eloquently conveyed his pride in his achievement, and his conviction that there are things in life just as important as achievement.

This is intensely personal poetry. It is also highly literary. In *Poems* 11, *Furi et Aureli, comites Catulli*, Catullus addresses two of his acquaintances, taking fourteen lines to assure them that he is confident that they would go with him to any of eight different remote and dangerous places in the far east, south, and north. He then asks them to take a filthy message to his estranged mistress. Horace's surprise is in a different style. Not for him the frenetic passions and recriminations of the poetic lover, and not a long list of distant places—he names only three but suggests there are many more by ending, here and only here in the odes, two consecutive lines with the word *et*. His Septimius may be ready to go to the barbarous south, the violent west, or anywhere else with him but what Horace wants is nothing so melodramatic, simply a quiet, civilized, and contented life in the Italian countryside. This poem is a direct and polemical allusion to Catullus 11, just as 1. 16 was a direct and polemical allusion to Catullus 36 (West 1995*a*: 80–1).

It is also a reply to Horace's friend, Virgil, the great poet of the 20s BC. Every Roman with any interest in poetry would have known about the old man who kept bees under the citadel of Tarentum, founded by the Spartans of whom Oebalus was a legendary king and where Virgil, an inveterate etymologizer, played in his own way with the milky river Galaesus, by calling it black:

> Namque sub Oebaliae memini me turribus arcis
> qua niger umectat flaventia culta Galaesus
> Corycium vidisse senem, cui pauca relicta
> iugera ruris erant, nec fertilis illa iuvencis
> nec pecori opportuna seges nec commoda Baccho.
>
> (Virgil, *Georgics* 4. 125–9)

> Under the towers of Oebalus' citadel
> where black Galaesus laves the golden fields
> I saw an old Corycian who had a few acres of waste land,
> and these not fertile enough to plough with oxen,
> not suitable for flocks, and not right for vines.

This was the first and unforgettable mention of the Galaesus in surviving Latin literature, and now, half a dozen years later, we have it again in association with old age, honey, the citadel of Tarentum ('citadels' in Horace), and a Spartan king, and in each poem Tarentum is taken as a model of serene life in the country. Horace corrects Catullus. He also corrects Virgil, much more gently. He may be straightening out Virgil's etymologizing by making the Galaesus sweet for sheep; he may be hinting at an alternative foundation-myth which gives the credit to Phalanthus rather than Oebalus; but certainly, he is making it clear that not all the land in sight of the towers of Tarentum is unfit for the plough, for sheep, and for vines. On the contrary he praises its honey, its olives, its sheep, and lastly, in line 20, its wine, a factor of crucial importance in retirement. The clinching argument, however, is Horace's direct contradiction of Virgil's assessment of the climate of the region:

> et cum tristis hiems etiamnum frigore saxa
> rumperet et glacie cursus frenaret aquarum,
> ille comam mollis iam tondebat hyacinthi
> aestatem increpitans seram Zephyrosque morantis.
>
> (Virgil, *Georgics* 4. 135–8)

> and when grim winter was still cracking the rocks
> with cold and reining in the running rivers with ice,
> he would already be shearing the soft fleece of the hyacinth,
> grumbling at summer for being late and Zephyrs for being slow.

It is as though Horace is joining his friend Virgil in praise of the district, but making it clear that Virgil has maligned its long springs and warm winters. Horace has no intention of going there to labour like the old Corycian in order to coax abundance from a reluctant soil, but rather to enjoy in comfortable retirement the gentle climate and the supreme quality of the local produce.

With their usual immense learning Nisbet and Hubbard show that this ode is like many earlier poems in Greek and Latin. It praises a locality, for instance, in standard terms, mentioning its founder, its trees, produce, rivers, and sheep. It even considers an option between two localities and, in the context of friendship, thinks of death; 'Horace's mellow and harmonious description of Tarentum seems delightfully adapted to its subject, but it is written within an idealising literary tradition.' Why 'seems'? Why 'but'? Such sentiments belong to life as well as to literature. In *Odes* 4. 2. 31 and 4. 3. 10 published ten years later, Horace will be writing as though he lives and works in Tibur. Perhaps in the 20s he and Septimius were already talking about properties in the two places.

This seems to be a modest and simple poem, speaking in quiet, resigned tones of retirement and death and the delights of Italy. And yet it carries a power which is peculiarly Horatian. The most valuable steps in analysing this power were made by Klingner (285–9), who observed the concentration of opposites in the poem. Septimius is ready to go with Horace to three places notable (*a*) for remoteness, (*b*) for refusal to accept Roman rule, and (*c*) for barbarity and a wild sea. This offer Horace rejects in the first two words of the second stanza. *Tibur Argeo* tells us that he prefers the Italian town of Tibur founded by a Greek from Argos, and then proceeds to make it plain that he is tired of (*c*) the sea, (*a*) travel to distant places (Gades is at the western limit of the world) and (*b*) warfare.

In the third stanza, too, the spark comes from contrasts: the wild Mauretanian sea gives way to the sweet water of a river with sheep on its banks; the suburbanity of Tibur and its famous cataract is replaced by a remote rural district with a pleasant river. This contrast is pointed by the relationship between the first line of the Tibur stanza, 'Tibur, founded by the Argive settler' answered by the end of the Tarentum stanza, 'the countryside ruled over by the Laconian Phalanthus', *Tibur Argeo positum colono*, answered by *regnata . . . Laconi rura Phalantho*. We now see that Tarentum, a Greek colony on Italian soil, unites the best of both Greek and Roman. It was founded by a Spartan and it rivals Athens for its honey, while it is equal to the best of the Italian for its olives and its wine. The whole of the Tarentum theme is defined by the lines 13–14, *ille terrarum mihi . . . angulus*, 'that corner of the earth for me', picked up by *ille te mecum locus* in line 21, 'That you with me place', to preserve the eloquent Latin word order. This last phrase also looks back to the opening of the poem, 'Septimius, who would go with me to Cadiz', *Septimi Gades aditure mecum* and binds it all together as question and answer. Even the citadels of line 22 are part of this accumulation of structural contrasts. Horace is weary of war, so now he will be putting these military installations to proper use as something pleasing and comforting to look up at from his rural paradise. The poem begins and ends with the value of friendship.

We expect such subtleties of tone from Horace. We can catch some of the richness and delicacy of his allusions, the telling details, the playful learning, the vivid sensory stimuli, the shrewd response to his poetic predecessors, even some of the music of his verse, but he has another gift, even more difficult to discuss—this taut, intelligent economy of mind. Pure Horace.

Among those who have enjoyed him is the Roman satirist Petronius. At the ludicrous dinner put on by the *nouveau riche* Trimalchio, we read:

> Trimalchio now looked over to us with a kindly face and said, 'If you don't like the wine, I'll change it. It's up to you to enjoy it. Thank the gods, I don't buy it, but nowadays everything that tickles the tastebuds grows on my estate near the city. I don't know it yet. They tell me it's on the boundaries between the Tarraciniensians and the Tarentines (*dicitur confine esse Tarraciniensibus et Tarentinis*). I want to add Sicily now to my little bits of land so that when I take a fancy to go to Africa I can sail there without leaving my own estate'. (Petronius, *Satiricon* 48. 1–3)

There are three jokes here all connected with Horace. The first is the unmistakable allusion to *Satires* 2. 8. 16–18, where another *nouveau riche* host Nasidienus says, 'If Alban or Falernian would please you better than what I've put on the table, Maecenas, we've got them both' and Horace comments *divitias miseras*, 'It's no fun being rich'. The third is the reference to the mania of Roman landowners for joining up their properties, as satirized in *Odes* 2. 2. 10–12, where Horace's example of joining Carthago to Nova Carthago is almost as absurd as Trimalchio's notion of crossing Sicily without leaving his own estate.

So much is obvious but the second joke has been misunderstood (West 1996*b*). Commentators have observed that Tarracina (modern Terracina), on the coast of Latium half-way between Rome and Naples, is so far from Tarentum in the arch of the foot of Italy that Nasidienus is simply showing his boastfulness and ignorance. 'Le rapprochement de Terracine et Tarente', writes Ernout, 'montre que la géographie de Trimalcion est assez confusé.' But there is more to it than that. Terracina is within walking distance of the vineyards which grew the grapes for Caecuban, and just to the west of the other areas which produced the great wines of Italy in Horace's day—Calenian, Falernian, Formian, and Massic. But to get the point we have to remember that in the fifth stanza of *Odes* 2. 6 Horace claims that the wines of Tarentum are as good as Falernian. Trimalchio is shaky on his Latin (he says *Tarraciniensibus* instead of *Tarracinensibus*), grossly ignorant of Italian geography, and also a wine snob. He vaguely remembers his Horace and he knows, or half knows, that Horace's favourite wines came not only from the Tarracina area but also from Tarentum. The point he is trying to make is that his wines are as good as Horace's. Petronius has managed to tickle the memories of his sophisticated readers by reminding them of Horace three times in half a dozen lines of Latin.

These three intertextual jokes in Petronius remind us that Horace's mind was saturated with previous literature in Greek and in Latin, and he used his recollections of that reading in writing his own poems. We have seen this many times—in the historical tones of 2. 1, the epic parody of 2. 4, the play with several different Greek poets in 2. 5 and 2. 6, including implicit judgements on Anacreon and Sappho, and an attempt to improve upon Catullus and to disagree more good-humouredly with Virgil. Evidence of Horace's use of past literature has been collected and usefully explored by centuries of scholarship, and of these findings Nisbet and Hubbard provide the best repository, enriched by their own learning and shrewd judgement.

Since their commentaries appeared in 1970 and 1978 intertextuality has been invented. In the essays in this book I have avoided theory.

Writings on literary theory are so complex, obscure, and abstract that they are of no help in the understanding of Horace. The third edition of the *Oxford Classical Dictionary* (1997) gives a brief introduction to intertextuality by some of the leading figures in the field, and would therefore be expected to provide a clear and authoritative starting-point for the study of this phenomenon.

Under the word 'Intertextuality' we are referred to *Imitatio*, and that article, by Conte and Most, begins with a definition. *Imitatio* is said to be 'the study and conspicuous deployment of features recognizably characteristic of a canonical author's style or content, so as to define one's own generic affiliation'. In this formulation 'study' is unnecessary, probably wrong—a writer might well practise *imitatio* without study; Horace did not need to study for *Odes* 2. 5. 14–15 where he took one of the most famous lines about love in the poems of Sappho and applied it to livestock. 'Conspicuous', too, is unnecessary. If a feature is '*recognisably* characteristic', there is no need to say that it is 'conspicuous'. Another unsatisfactory stipulation is the word 'canonical'. There is no shortage of examples of poets who practise *imitatio* of uncanonical writers. The final element in the definition, 'so as to define one's own generic affiliation' is another stumbling-block. If 'so as to' is meant to indicate purpose, we are being asked to accept an explanation of the motives of poets which is totally absurd, and is rendered even more useless by the statement under 'Genre' by the same two authors that 'theory of genre as such is quite lacking in antiquity'.

This may all seem to be pedantic, but intertextuality is a field where most of the writing is muddled and unreadable, and here, in a definition standing in a separate paragraph at the beginning of an entry in a central reference work, we can surely ask for exactness. The words are sober and clear by the standards of writing in this field, and yet this analysis shows how even here the thinking is so loose that it is difficult to make sense of the writing.

We look across now to the article 'Literary Theory and Classical Studies' by D. P. and P. G. Fowler, where, on page 872, there is a paragraph explicitly on intertextuality. Here we read, 'because all texts participate in literary systems, all texts (and not only literary ones) are always already of necessity shot through with the presence of other texts. A text which did not participate in any system in this way would be literally unreadable, since we would have no possible codes with which to decipher it. Authors cannot decide whether to be allusive: whatever they intend, their texts will be read against the "matrix of possibilities" created by other texts.' There is a basic truth underlying this formulation. It seems to be saying that texts use language and that readers' understanding of language is based upon their experience of it. *If* this is what is being said, it is true but so vapid and obvious that it is not worth saying, and it is totally irrelevant to the task of understanding poetry. Why then does it sound so important? Essentially, the elevation of style comes from the use of metaphor. 'Texts participate' is a fine phrase, but they do not. Texts are inert. They are marks on a flat surface. It is the reader who participates, not the text. But that is not a valuable statement. And so on with 'texts already of necessity shot through with the presence of other texts'. Already? Shot through? Presence? The figurative language conceals the banality of the thought.

The case for intertextuality is put later in the paragraph, 'it gave a powerful impetus to studies of literary relationships which moved beyond comparing and contrasting related passages to an insight into how the presence of earlier texts, if recognised by a critic, can radically affect interpretation'. There has been a huge effort over centuries to collect parallel passages and admittedly many of the collections do not put the material to use. But this is no adverse criticism. These linguistic data may well have been pondered in helping the collecting scholar to refine his understanding of the target text, but even if they have had no such discernible effect, they may still be useful. The material is now there in the scholarly tradition for others to use and be grateful for. The surprise is that the writers of this reference article can claim that intertextuality gave an impetus to this technique of gaining insight into how the presence of

---

VII

O saepe mecum tempus in ultimum
deducte Bruto militiae duce,
quis te redonavit Quiritem
dis patriis Italoque caelo,

Pompei, meorum prime sodalium?
cum quo morantem saepe diem mero
fregi coronatus nitentis
malobathro Syrio capillos.

earlier texts can radically affect interpretation. Comparison and contrast of texts is a basic method of teaching and it is what scholars have tried to do throughout the centuries (without of course the metaphor of the presence of texts). Intertextuality cannot claim credit for this. Examples are legion but we need to look no further than Knauer's great work on the *Aeneid* and Nisbet and Hubbard's commentaries on Horace to find passage after passage illuminated by such comparisons. No doubt some intertextualists have improved our understanding of texts, but not as intertextualists. These two articles in the *Oxford Classical Dictionary* are comparatively comprehensible, but in full flow this approach produces slack reasoning, jargon, and pretentious, obscurantist writing. Some of it is so difficult to read that serious scholars do not waste their time on it and it is impossible to avoid the suspicion that even other intertextualists do not understand it. It is therefore acclaimed unjudged, because it is an utterance in the idiom. The Fowlers end their article by claiming that intertextuality is central to the revaluation of the Flavian epicists, 'viewed not as servile imitators of Virgil, but as machines for producing striking intertextual complexities'.

'Une maison est une machine-à-habiter', wrote Le Corbusier in 1923, and this was a shrewd, timely, and meaningful image, intertextually related, no doubt, to the 'Sitzmaschine' designed by Josef Hofmann and discussed by C. and P. Fiell in 'Modern Chairs'. Hofmann and Le Corbusier make ergonomic sense, but to call Statius a machine for producing striking intertextual complexities is clever, but silly.

VII

You and I have often been led to the edge
of doom with Brutus in command,
    and now who has made you a Roman again
        and restored you to your fathers' gods and Italian skies,

O Pompeius, first of my friends, with whom
I so often broke into the lagging day with neat wine,
    head garlanded and hair sleek
        with Syrian malobathrum?

tecum Philippos et celerem fugam
sensi relicta non bene parmula,
cum fracta virtus, et minaces
turpe solum tetigere mento.

sed me per hostis Mercurius celer
denso paventem sustulit aere;
te rursus in bellum resorbens
unda fretis tulit aestuosis.

ergo obligatam redde Iovi dapem
longaque fessum militia latus
depone sub lauru mea, nec
parce cadis tibi destinatis.

oblivioso levia Massico
ciboria exple; funde capacibus
unguenta de conchis. quis udo
deproperare apio coronas

curatve myrto? quem Venus arbitrum
dicet bibendi? non ego sanius
bacchabor Edonis: recepto
dulce mihi furere est amico.

This is a political poem. Caesar was assassinated in 44 BC by the conspirators led by Brutus and Cassius. In 42 Brutus was in Athens and recruited young Horace and presumably his student friend Pompeius, otherwise unknown, to serve in the republican army which was destroyed by Antony and Octavian at Philippi. After the defeat Horace made peace with the victors and built his life as a poet and servant of the regime, but Pompeius continued the struggle, the sea metaphor in lines 15–16 hinting that he served with Sextus Pompeius (perhaps a member of the same family) until his fleet was destroyed at the battle of Mylae in 36 BC. Thereafter he may have gone east with others who escaped, fought for Antony until the battle of Actium in 31, and eventually been spared by Octavian in 30 BC along with others (Velleius, 2. 86. 2 and Dio, 51. 16. 1). The answer to the opening question is 'Octavian' and this poem is a tribute to the clemency which was a much advertised feature of Augustan policy, as claimed by Augustus himself in his *Res Gestae* 3. 1, and celebrated for example by Velleius in the chapter just cited. It would have been Octavian who restored Pompeius to the roll of Roman citizens (*Quirites* in line 3 is the traditional emotive term) and we should remem-

With you I knew Philippi and speedy flight,
leaving my little shield behind, shame to say,
when virtue snapped and the chins
of blusterers touched the base earth.

I panicked, but swift Mercury carried me off
in a dense mist through the enemy ranks,
while a wave sucked you back into war
and swept you along in a boiling sea.

So pay to Jupiter the feast that was vowed,
lay down your body weary with campaigning
here under my laurel tree, and have no mercy
on the casks of wine I have reserved for you.

Fill up the polished Egyptian cups with Massic
for forgetfulness and pour fragrant oils from full shells.
Whose business is it to run
for garlands of moist celery

and myrtle? Whom will Venus choose as master
of the wine? I shall run wild as any Edonian
at her Bacchic orgies. My friend is back.
What joy to go mad!

ber that Augustus attached such importance to his revision of the citizen roll in 28 BC that he commemorated it thirty-two years later in the official record of his life's achievements, *Res Gestae* 8. 2, 'In my sixth consulship with Marcus Agrippa as colleague, I carried out a census of the people. I performed a *lustrum* after a lapse of forty-two years, at which 4,063,000 Roman citizens were registered.' (A *lustrum* was a ceremony of purification conducted by the censors, in theory every five years.)

This is not only a political poem. It is also warmly personal. Horace and Pompeius had been young army officers together, and probably before that students together, and such friendships often survive decades of separation. In the first five lines of the poem Horace welcomes his long-lost friend back into the fold. Pompeius had often, *saepe*, shared danger with him, *mecum*, and this note is struck again at lines 5–6, 9, 13–16, and 19–20. Horace is delighted to think that his old friend is a Roman citizen again, back in his home with his ancestral gods and under the skies of Italy after long and dangerous years abroad. Pompeius is called the first of his friends, and scholars needlessly debate whether the adjective means first in value or first in time. There can be no doubt, however, of the overtones of the noun *sodalium*, 'drinking companions' and it sets Horace off on a reminiscence of the wild days they spent together so long ago in Greece, when they went against respectable Roman practice by starting to drink during the day, and by drinking their wine neat. A cheerful touch of Horatian surrealism comes at the thought of using wine to split a day. Romans would normally put fragrant oils in their hair at symposia. The oil used by Horace, however, was no ordinary oil, but an exotic Syrian unguent from the cinnamon tree, *cinnamomum tamala*, never mentioned in any other Roman poetry that survives, but perhaps available to the gilded youth in Athens in 44–42 BC. The sleekness of Horace's hair in those distant days is another smile between the friends. Three years later, in 20 BC, in *Epistles* 1. 20. 24, Horace describes his hair as prematurely grey.

In *Satires* 1. 6. 48 Horace told us that he had been a military tribune, using perhaps a slight exaggeration for the sake of the poem in saying that he commanded a Roman legion. (Military tribunes were second in command to the legate, and could take command in his absence.) In this poem his purposes are different. Here he minimizes his part in the battle, saying that he was quick to run away, leaving his little shield behind not very creditably, *non bene*. The self-deflation is tact. Pompeius had continued to fight on the wrong side. To distract the reader, and Pompeius, from this painful fact, Horace presents himself as a coward here and with *paventem* in line 14, but being Horace, he manages to be boastful and self-deprecating at one and the same time. When he began to write these odes there was a canon of nine great lyric poets, all of them Greek, including Alcaeus and Anacreon, who threw away their shields on the field of battle. Now Horace has followed this august Greek tradition and so acquired a qualification to entitle his Latin verses to be enrolled in the Greek canon. Then, like Aeneas and Hector, he is whisked off the battlefield, not by Apollo (*Iliad* 5. 344 and 20. 443) or Poseidon (*Iliad* 20. 325) but by Mercury, a much less serious god (so *Odes* 1. 10). But even so, the divine messenger shows a useful turn of speed in line 13 as he does for Horace what the great gods do for real heroes. This mock-heroic treatment serves to show that Horace appreciates how lucky he has been and how different life has been for his friend Pompeius, sucked back into war by the undertow of a storm wave. Not a whisper of criticism for his choosing the wrong side. The differences are that he was caught by a power that no man could resist and that Horace was a coward.

When a Roman came back from a journey, as for example at 1. 36, an early task was to pay the vows that had been made for his safe return, and almost as urgent would be the need to hold a banquet and a symposium. This poem thus ends with its second symposium and it seems that the mature Horace is trying in changed circumstances, in Rome in peacetime instead of on campaign in Greece, to replicate their earlier extravaganza and thus demonstrate to his friend that nothing has changed between them. But this time the party is, in telling ways, a little more respectable and a little more Roman. For one thing it is the payment of a vow to Jupiter. For another this is not now adolescent high spirits, but an outburst of joy at the return of a friend who has suffered in wars that Horace has avoided. Now Horace has a garden with a laurel tree, as befits a poet, and a drama comes to life as he commands Pompeius in mock-military terms to have no mercy on the casks laid down specially for him. They will drink good Italian Massic, but from *ciboria*, goblets in the shape of the seed-box of the Egyptian bean, in fact a giant water lily, *Nelumpium speciosum*. Such goblets appear in Greek symposia (Athenaeus, 11. 477) but only here in surviving Latin. Perhaps this is another sentimental reminder to Pompeius of their days in Greece (or even in Egypt, if we guess that Pompeius followed Antony and Cleopatra to their last days in Alexandria). There will be no shortage of unguents, but not this time rare Syrian malobathrum. Horace gives a cheerful shout to get some slave or other to run and get garlands, moist presumably because they are celery fresh from the side of a stream flowing through Horace's garden. The myrtle, plant of Venus, suggests that wine will lead to love, as it no doubt did in the days of studenting and soldiering in Greece, and, sure enough, Venus comes pat, in her role as the highest throw of the dice, to appoint the master of the wine. But at a symposium nobody will fail to think of her other role. Bacchus will be worshipped and as his orgiastic rites, which originated in Thrace, famously involved the activities of frenzied Maenads, Horace will be as frenzied as the Edonians, a Thracian tribe in whose territory was fought the fateful battle of Philippi. In the outburst of commands, rhetorical questions, and wild extravagances which end the poem, there is total enjambement. Every sentence ends in the middle of a line to give an impression of the intensity of Horace's feelings. The poem which began with Pompeius as a drinking companion ends with Pompeius as a friend. It is a notable display of strategies of affection, but Horace is still aware of the political realities, and careful not to run the risk of offending his Augustan patrons.

We have already caught the tribute to Augustus' clemency in the first stanza. We may also catch with Moles a hint of Brutus' well-known incompetence as a general when we hear that he often led his men to the edge of the doom, literally 'to the last time', *tempus ad ultimum*. Moles also senses in the second stanza a suggestion that the republican army was staffed by young men who did not respect the disciplines of war, and in the third that the philosophical *virtus* of Brutus, much vaunted by his contemporaries and by himself, was a brittle virtue, that the republicans were arrogant, threatening, *minaces* (Appian, 4. 125), and that there is a reminder in line 12 when their faces are rubbed in the dirt, that those

---

VIII

ULLA si iuris tibi peierati
poena, Barine, nocuisset umquam,
dente si nigro fieres vel uno
    turpior ungui,

crederem. sed tu, simul obligasti
perfidum votis caput, enitescis
pulchrior multo iuvenumque prodis
    publica cura.

expedit matris cineres opertos
fallere et toto taciturna noctis
signa cum caelo gelidaque divos
    morte carentis.

ridet hoc, inquam, Venus ipsa, rident
simplices Nymphae, ferus et Cupido,
semper ardentis acuens sagittas
    cote cruenta.

adde quod pubes tibi crescit omnis,
servitus crescit nova, nec priores
impiae tectum dominae relinquunt,
    saepe minati.

te suis matres metuunt iuvencis,
te senes parci, miseraeque nuper
virgines nuptae, tua ne retardet
    aura maritos.

who had once been threatening were forced in the end to submit to Antony and Octavian (Appian, 4. 135).

Horace has hunted with the hounds and run with the hare, producing a testament of loyalty not only to an old friend but also to current friends and benefactors. As Syndikus (386) says, 'this freedom of speech does as much honour to Augustus as it does to the poet'.

VIII

If you had ever suffered any punishment
for perjury, Barine, if you were uglier
by a black tooth or a speck of white
  on one fingernail,

I would believe. But the minute you pledge
your lying self, your beauty shines the brighter,
and you walk the streets a public menace
  to young men.

It pays you to swear false oaths by the ashes
of your mother in her tomb, by the silent stars of night,
sky and all, and by the gods who never feel
  the chill of death.

Venus herself, I do declare, laughs at this,
the guileless nymphs laugh at it, and heartless Cupid,
forever sharpening burning arrows on his whetstone
  dripping with blood.

Add to the case that all the young are growing up for you,
new slaves are growing, and the old ones
never leave the house of their impious mistress,
  for all their threats.

Mothers are afraid of you for the sake of their young bullocks,
close-fisted old men too, and unhappy virgin brides,
in case their husbands catch your scent
  and come home late.

This is not a difficult poem, but the first sentence is surprising. At the risk of making a mountain out of a speck of white, we might analyse the logic as follows. Barine is offering to swear that she will truly love Horace. Horace is sceptical, because he knows that she has betrayed many lovers before him and not suffered for it. Her beauty is still unflawed. Why Horace would believe her if there were a speck of white on one of her fingernails, is not immediately obvious. To make sense of this statement, we have to supply an unstated conclusion. Since she lies and never suffers, she must have some dispensation which exempts her from the normal punishments for dishonesty. If Horace had ever seen the minutest blemish on her body, he would deduce that there was no such dispensation, and therefore, that, on occasion, she might possibly be telling the truth.

This analysis is even more ponderous than it seems. There is no speck of white in the Latin, which literally says 'if you were uglier by a black tooth or by one nail'. The normal way to understand this would be to borrow 'one' from the nail to the tooth and borrow 'black' from the tooth to the nail, so that Barine would have one black tooth and one black nail. Against this there must be cited the ancient superstition that a speck of white on a fingernail is a sign of dishonesty. The Greeks called such specks 'lovers', *erastai*, or 'lies', *pseude* (Alexander of Aphrodisias, *Problemata*, 14). There is another argument. A black mark on Barine's fingernail could have been caused if she had hit it with a hammer or caught it in a door. A white mark on a nail would have had no known material cause and could have been taken to demonstrate the displeasure of the gods. The mark, therefore, must be white.

Translations which fail to provide the sense are failing the poet. Translations which provide explanations in the text are failing the poet by their officiousness, and in this case spoiling the ponderous symmetry of the Latin: 'any' and 'every' framing the first two lines, and 'tooth' and 'nail' framing lines 3–4; *Ulla si* beginning the first line, picked up by *dente si* beginning the third. Translations always fail.

Part of the fun in the first two stanzas lies in the parody of legal language. Punishment (*poena*), law (*ius*) in the phrase *iuris perierati*, harm (*nocuisset*), and in line 7 *caput*, the head, meaning the person, the life—all of these terms recur frequently in the surviving fragments of the Twelve Tables, the ancient basis of Roman law, which schoolboys had to learn by heart in Cicero's day (*De Legibus* 2. 23. 59). Horace's contemporary readers would have caught the flavour of these two stanzas and realized that this is not a serious poem. Even the conditional clause in lines 2–4 may add a little legal spice. The first thirty-two words of the Twelve Tables include five conditional clauses, starting with 'If [a plaintiff] summons [a defendant] to law, he shall go', *Si in ius vocat,* [*ito*]. In line 5 of the ode *obligatam* is also a technical term of the law, as in the passages cited in the *Oxford Latin Dictionary*. Later, at line 17, *adde quod* is a pedantic connective. We can easily imagine a barrister mouthing it. In Horace these technicalities are freely handled, notably the words translated as 'perjury' in the first line. An oath in Latin is *ius iurandum*, literally 'a law requiring to be sworn'. Horace's phrase posits a phrase attested nowhere else, *ius peieratum*, 'a law having been perjured'. Perhaps it is a mischievous invention.

There are sense pauses at the end of each stanza of this poem except the first—'if even a speck of white showed on one fingernail', what then? The single word *crederem*, 'I would believe' breaks into the following stanza. The placing of the word gives it great emphasis and the emphasis warns us not to believe it. It would take more than a blemish on a fingernail to make Horace believe in Barine. This poem celebrates her beauty, not her capacity for fidelity. The stanza ends with a pun. The word *cura* usually refers to anxiety, but in the language of the lover in Latin elegy it often refers to love. It was, for example, lazy Ovid's love for a pretty girl which drove him into Cupid's camp at *Amores* 1. 9. 43, *impulit ignavum formosae cura puellae*. So here the one word *cura* suggests that she is the darling of young men and at the same time a matter of public concern, as will be explained at the end of the poem.

Each of the first two stanzas has included two pairs. They are followed by four stanzas, each of which is a triad. In lines 9–12 mother, stars, and gods are involved as Horace builds up the case against Barine. Here, as in 2. 6 (see pp. 44–5) some of the poetic energy comes from contrasts, not all of them explicit. Her mother is dead; the gods live for ever. Her mother's ashes are hidden, *opertos*, in her tomb; the stars are visible. The ashes of her mother are cold; the stars are fire, and the gods never know the chill of death. The stars are silent when Barine utters her vows, but they see what is furtive.

Venus, the Nymphs, and Cupid make up the next triad. In Greek and Latin poetry the god who usually laughs when lovers break their oaths in Jupiter. Here Venus is the deity who laughs because a woman is betraying a man. Jupiter would not find this so amusing. It is surprising also that guileless Nymphs should laugh at deceit, particularly because the adjective *simplex* often connotes truthfulness. But Nymphs are female. Even guileless, truthful girls are amused by Barine's virtuosity. Cupid presumably makes up the three because he plays tricks on both sexes. He is, of course, cruel, and Horace provides a vivid description of him in six words of Latin. His whetstone is bloody because arrows are sharpened on it while they are still wet with the blood of their previous victim; and these arrows are blazing, *ardentes*, because of the ardour of the love they inflict and the sparks showering from the whetstone. These arrows of Cupid are the stock-in-trade of Hellenistic and Roman love poets, for whom love is often a fire and Cupid's arrows are fiery missiles. His whetstone, too, appears in literature and in art. Nisbet and Hubbard cite many occurrences of all of these, and a couple of blood on arrows. An extra resonance is that Rome had been at war throughout Horace's lifetime and some of his readers would have seen burning arrows flying onto thatched roofs in besieged cities. To combine all these elements into one concentrated picture and have Cupid laughing as he works, shows Horace characteristically using familiar material to produce his own picture.

In line 17 the young men are growing up for her, and Horace immediately in the line that follows explains this strange statement in terms of the Slavery of Love, *Servitium Amoris* (see Lyne 1980: 78–81, and an interesting note by McKeown on Ovid, *Amores* 1. 3. 5). This slavery, not at all Horace's chosen way of love, is a common concept in the elegiac poets, and he mocks it by the repetition of growing in lines 17–18, which makes it sound like a queue waiting to join Barine's entourage. The old hands are also ridiculous. They are always threatening to leave, but they never do. Notice again the delicious Sapphic effect (see on 2. 4) here and in every short line in this poem.

Mothers, old men, and brides are the last triad. The second item need not detain us. Most Roman comedies star stingy old men afraid that their lovelorn sons are squandering their patrimony. The mothers are afraid for their bullocks. As so often in Horace, the ground for an astonishing proposition has been prepared in a previous ode. In 2. 5. 6–8 a young girl is seen as a heifer and young men as bullocks. This striking metaphor sets the stage for the last surprise. Barine's *aura* (breeze, odour, effluence, glow), which is in some danger of retarding the newly married husband, could be a contrary breeze if this were a nautical metaphor; or it could refer to the glow radiating from her (we have heard about it in line 6), but *aura* usually means 'breeze', and refers to light only in rare and special circumstances. Virgil's 'breath of gold', *aura auri*, for the Golden Bough in *Aeneid* 6. 204 is unparalleled, 'a Virgilian marvel' (Austin ad loc.), a marvel which is helped by the gentle breeze, *leni vento*, which makes the metal of the Golden Bough rustle at line 209. But in this context, after the mention of bullocks, the first thing a reader must think of is the odour emanating from her. This could be her perfume but the Romans knew, from Virgil, *Georgics* 3. 250–1 if not directly, that bullocks are thrilled by the smell of cows. To see a bull arriving at a farm and being released into new territory, as he raises his great nostrils to the sky and loudly, snortingly, sniffs the air, leaves no doubt that he is susceptible to the odour. Another twist in this sentence is that the unhappy women, though newly married, are still *virgines*. Such is the power of Barine. Griffin (184) rejects this interpretation of *aura* and calls it a lapse of taste by Nisbet and Hubbard, but whether we like it or not, after *iuvencis* bullocks in line 21 and the sustained image in 2. 5 there may be a whiff of perfume, but there is no doubt about the smell of cows.

There is one other Horatian marvel in this last stanza. Each of the clauses begins with the second-person pronoun or adjective, *te . . . te . . . tua*, a standard feature of the hymn style in Horace and elsewhere, as exemplified in the last stanza of 1. 12, whose three clauses addressing Jupiter begin *te . . . tu . . . tu* (see the index to West (1995*a*) under 'Kletic hymn'). It seems that Horace is saying these slightly scandalous things about Barine in devout religious terms. This, in turn, may throw the mind back to line 17, 'the young are growing for you', *pubes tibi crescit*. Again Horace may provide an explanation of his own flight of fancy. In 3. 23. 11–13 a sacrificial victim is growing in Alban pastures, *crescit Albanis in herbis victima*. The young would then be the victims fattening for sacrifice and Barine would be the goddess, egged on by the amused deities of the fourth stanza.

This poem has not been much liked. Wickham objects to 'the offensive metaphor' with which it ends and Copley (160) thought it 'even worse than the worst of Catullus', displaying 'an ugly, vicious temper, in place of Catullus' honest, if misguided, attempts at humour'. There would be some weight in these opinions if this were a full-blown dramatic monologue which posited silent contributions from a person addressed. But it reads differently. It is an indictment which inverts the common motif whereby a betrayed female rages about the falsity of her lover, and twists stock arguments of love poetry to have fun by imagining a man suffering from the dishonesty of a flawlessly beautiful woman. Could it be that the poem is not a demonstration of an ugly, vicious temper, but a *jeu d'esprit* conveying a touch of admiration for this character Horace has created? Normally we cannot say whether Horace gives a true account of his relationships with the women in the odes, or indeed whether such women even existed. Agnosticism is the rule. But here it can surely be broken. Horace did not say these things to any woman. Barine is not a credible person, but a poetic creation. She never existed.

This note began by saying that 2. 8 is not a difficult poem. But it is pure Horace in its density, its tonal modulations, its internal interactions, its revitalization of familiar material, its unexpected twists, its humour, its taste for danger, its imagery, and its elusiveness.

It raises a question of principle, the difficulty of recognizing puns. Internal cross-references, as analysed above for the third stanza for instance, are so numerous that scholars have been encouraged to see some which the poet is unlikely to have intended and contemporary readers are unlikely to have perceived. Nisbet and Hubbard, for instance, note that *obligare*, to bind, to pledge, is used by Seneca, *De Ira* 3. 11. 4 of blindfolding the eyes, and they therefore connect the binding of the head, *caput*, with the glow in that same line—'when you bind your head, you shine', *simul obligasti caput enitescis*. This I would reject, because in this context the essential meaning, 'you pledge yourself', is so immediately apparent and blindfolding is so remote, that readers could not be expected to think of it. Similarly, in line 10 *fallere* means 'to cheat' but Nisbet and Hubbard invoke also its other meaning, 'to escape notice', suggesting that there is tension in Barine not being seen by her mother's ashes which are hidden, *opertos*. Again, this seems to be forced. The obvi-

---

IX

NON semper imbres nubibus hispidos
manant in agros aut mare Caspium
  vexant inaequales procellae
    usque, nec Armeniis in oris,

amice Valgi, stat glacies iners
mensis per omnis aut Aquilonibus
  querqueta Gargani laborant
    et foliis viduantur orni:

tu semper urges flebilibus modis
Mysten ademptum, nec tibi Vespero
  surgente decedunt amores
    nec rapidum fugiente solem.

ous sense of *fallere* in this context, like the obvious sense of *obligasti* above, is so commanding here that it does not seem likely that many Roman readers would have called in these extra possibilities which make poor and unappealing sense. 'To escape the notice of what is hidden' seems to be a footling idea. Similarly, Nisbet and Hubbard suggest the possibility of *double entendre* at the first word of the third stanza. *Expedit*, it pays, it profits, can also mean it frees, it releases. But again, in this context *expedit* is the salient and necessary sense—it pays Barine to swear falsely by her mother's ashes. Could any reader or listener, caught in the impetus of the sense, think of 'it' *releasing* Barine's mother? Surely not. What would 'it' be? And from what is Barine's dead mother being released? Another possible example of this tendency to overinterpret is the suggestion that there is a formal balance between *adde* and *crescit* in line 17, 'add to this the fact that the youth increases'. Except in slapstick, puns and interplays of this sort are dynamic only if each of the posited meanings is cogent or suggestive in the context, like *cura* in line 8. But if the main meaning leaps to the mind and is sufficient, and the suggested secondary meaning is a poor fit and does little for the wit, it is better not to step aside for it. But this is a treacherous area, where no footing is sure, and we are all likely to favour what we ourselves have detected.

IX

Rain is not always streaming down from clouds
on roughened fields, wild squalls
   are not forever vexing the Caspian Sea
      and not through every month of the year,

My dear friend Valgius, does ice stand motionless
on Armenian shores, nor do the oaks of Garganus
   labour in north winds, and ash trees are not always
      being widowed of their leaves.

But you are forever harassing your lost Mystes
with mournful melodies and your love never leaves you,
   not when Vesper rises,
      nor when he flees from the scorching sun.

at non ter aevo functus amabilem
ploravit omnis Antilochum senex
annos, nec impubem parentes
Troilon aut Phrygiae sorores

flevere semper. desine mollium
tandem querelarum, et potius nova
cantemus Augusti tropaea
Caesaris et rigidum Niphaten,

Medumque flumen gentibus additum
victis minores volvere vertices,
intraque praescriptum Gelonos
exiguis equitare campis.

At the end of the first book of the *Satires*, published a dozen years before these odes appeared in 23 BC, Horace names fifteen friends whom he would like to please with his poems. Numbers three to five on the list are Maecenas, Virgil, and Valgius. Valgius himself seems to have written several different types of poetry, including panegyric. A dozen lines of elegy survive and are edited by Courtney 287–90.

'Belinda smiled and all the world was gay', from Pope's *Rape of the Lock*, used to be a stock example of the pathetic fallacy, the notion that attributed feeling, *pathos*, to something that could not experience it. To make this figure work, there must be terms which can operate on either side of the line. So here, at the beginning of the Horace, *imbres*, showers, can be used of showers of tears; *nubes*, clouds, can be used of the clouds of gloom; *manant*, flow, of tears; *vexant*, *inaequales*, *procellae*, and *laborant* can all be applied to human passions, and *viduantur*, 'they are being widowed' suggests bereavement. So also, in this context, *hispidos*, rough, unkempt, may contribute to the pathetic fallacy. In view of the established Roman practice of neglecting one's toilet during mourning (see the *Oxford Latin Dictionary* under *squalor*, *sordes*, *sordidus*, *sordidatus*), *hispidos* may well be part of the argument of the poem. On the other hand editors point out that of the four storm-battered localities in the first two stanzas, three are named, the Caspian, Armenia, and Mount Garganus on the large spur on the Adriatic coast of Italy. They have therefore been attracted to Orelli's conjecture, *Istricos*, which would place the rain-soaked fields on the banks of the Danube, the Ister. This would give four geographical adjectives and very tidy Latin, but Horace is not always tidy. He sometimes surprises, and here the attempt to improve what the

Odes 2.9

But the old man who lived three lifetimes did not spend
all his years mourning his beloved Antilochus,
and the Phrygian parents and sisters
of young Troilus did not weep for him

for ever. Give over at last these soft complaints
and let us rather sing of the new trophies
of Caesar Augustus,
of the Niphates frozen hard,

of the Persian river joining its peoples in defeat
and lowering the crests of its rolling waves,
of the Geloni riding their horses
where permitted on their narrow plains.

manuscripts offer has destroyed a nuance which has a bearing on a vital question about this poem.

In line 9 Mystes has been taken away or lost, *ademptum*. Has he gone to a new lover? Has he left the district? Has he died? It seems that *hispidos*, like *viduantur*, has been leading us to think of death, and this is confirmed by the mournful melodies of line 10, *flebilibus modis*, which suggest that Valgius has been composing elegiac verses. Lines 10–12 confirm this deduction in that they would have reminded anyone reading this poem in Horace's day of the unforgettable cadences in which Virgil describes how Orpheus lamented his dead Eurydice as day came and as day departed, *te veniente die, te decedente canebat*, in *Georgics* 4. 466. The last indication that Mystes has died is in the two similes in lines 13–17. They offer broad hints that Mystes is like Antilochus in being *amabilem*, lovable; like Troilus in being *impubem*, young; and like both in being dead.

At this point we have to judge a suggestion put forward by Nisbet and Hubbard. They collect the allusions to Antilochus and Troilus in Homer and find that Horace has Homer in the forefront of his mind. Nestor loved his son, but ten years after the fall of Troy Telemachus found the old man serene in his palace, with sons sound in judgement and good with the spear (*Odyssey* 4. 210–11). We can understand also why Horace chooses Troilus. Priam, Hecuba, and their daughters had much to grieve them in the Trojan War, but not many of their bereavements can have touched them more poignantly than the death of the youngest son of the family. Nisbet and Hubbard, however, want to go further. They point out, citing Philostratus in the fourth century AD (*Imagines* 2. 7. 1), that 'later writers developed the erotic possibilities of the situation' for Antilochus. Troilus is praised for his beauty by Ibycus (282. 41–6) in the sixth century BC, and Phrynichus in the fifth (fragment 13) says that the light of love gleams on his crimson cheeks. Nisbet and Hubbard therefore suggest that there may be a malicious irony in calling Troilus *impubem*, in that there is a suggestion that he had not yet reached the age of sexual experience. There is surely humour in this poem, for example in the repeated stress on 'always' in the Latin of lines 1, 4, 6, 9, 10–12, 14–15, and 17. We may also detect a ghost of a smile in lines 11–12 where Horace has inverted Virgil's time-markers, so that Valgius remembers his love not from dawn to dusk but from dusk to dawn. There is also a bracing shock at the full stop in the middle of line 17, 'nobody grieves for ever. Stop at long last your soft complaints'.

Are we then to catch a hint of homosexual love in the similes in lines 13–17? In this matter there is no certainty. Horace is an elusive poet, but for me this suggestion is quite out of place. The similes are more effective, paradoxically more humorous, if their tone is grave, rather than sexually suggestive. The love and grief are the love and grief of parents and sisters. The humour comes not in sly hints, but in the contrast between epic nobility and Valgius' obsession with his boy lover.

Horace is famed for his tact in friendship. What manner of tact is it to tell a friend to stop mourning someone he loved and instead write panegyrics of Augustus? There is one theory which eases this difficulty and makes good Horatian sense of the ode. The nub of the poem is not Mystes, but poems that Valgius has been writing about him. Perhaps he died a long time ago. Perhaps, and this is very likely, he never existed, and Valgius has simply become stuck in a rut of elegiac lamentation for a name without a person. On this explanation Horace is teasing his friend (hence the many repetitions of 'always') and begging him to move to a different kind of writing, in fact to panegyric, which we know that he practised from *Panegyricus Messallae* 179–80. Valgius has probably already done what Horace is now advising him to do. 'Let *us* sing', he says to his friend, 'the military achievements of Augustus.' He then proceeds to do it himself.

He has already shown in these odes that he can praise the great without writing long epics, and he now sets out on a tour of the world which Augustus has conquered. First he surveys an eastern river, the Niphates, perhaps the Tigris (the reference may also be to a mountain, but the pathetic fallacy of imagining a snowy river (*niphas* is the Greek for snow) frozen with fear of Augustus is livelier and more meaningful than attributing rigidity to a mountain). Next the river of the Medes, the Euphrates, is chastened and lowers the crests of his waves. The statues of river-gods were carried on floats in Roman triumphs, and a subdued Euphrates appears with gentler waves in Augustus' triumph at the end of *Aeneid* 8, *Euphrates ibat iam mollior undis*. The Geloni of line 23 were Scythians, and Scythians were nomads on the move across the great plains of south Russia. In Seneca, *Oedipus* 478, Bacchus subdued the scattered Geloni, *ille dispersos domuit Gelonos*. It seems that Augustus also claimed credit for restricting the movements of these formidable horsemen. He certainly refers at *Res Gestae* 31 to an embassy which reached him from the Scythians in 25 BC and Horace must be singing the same song when he tells us in *Odes* 3. 8. 23–4 that the Scythians have unstrung their bows and are preparing to leave their plains,

> iam Scythae laxo meditantur arcu
>   cedere campis.

Horace has advised Valgius not to grieve for Mystes, and what he means is that he should stop writing doleful poems about him. This ode is not about Valgius' grief but about his writing.

It is a common practice in modern scholarship to interpret poems as though they are about poetry. In such 'metapoetic' interpretations statements about love, wine, flowers, and the simple life can easily be taken not to mean what they say, but to be declarations of the artistic programme of the poet. *Persicos odi apparatus*, 'I hate Persian paraphernalia' writes Horace to begin *Odes* 1. 38, the tiny poem which follows the great Cleopatra ode at the end of his first book, and Davis takes Persian to refer to 'a verbal *opus* which is large-scale and overblown'; *odi* 'is a way of excluding at the outset, an unsophisticated audience (*profanum vulgus*) before announcing an innovative poetic program' (*Odes* 3. 1. 1–4); *apparatus* draws a parallel between magnificent preparations for banquets and 'an ornate style of discourse'; and so on for almost every word in the poem until the last four, *sub arta vite bibentem*: 'In locating the quintessentially convivial gesture *sub arta vite* ("beneath the dense vine") Horace obliquely embraces the motif of shade, or protective *umbra*, which is the generative matrix of the lyric *carmen*.' On *bibentem* he writes, 'The poet leaves the reader with a symbolic distillation of the preponderant character of his convivial Muse.' The Latin speaks of Horace drinking wine.

Davis's approach is based upon the constant use of the pansemantic fallacy, by which any shade of meaning of a word can be thought to be active in any context (see West 1995*a*: 160–1). Of course dictionary work reveals that many of these words in 1. 38 can in certain contexts have the meaning posited by the metapoetic interpreter, but in this context Horace is telling his slave to bring him some wine without any fuss. The details of the poem are magical in their literal sense, charged with humour, affection, and individual humanity. The metapoetic interpretation is neither humane or individual, but a statement of literary intent, boringly like all the other metapoetic interpretations of Horatian odes.

X

Rectius vives, Licini, neque altum
semper urgendo neque, dum procellas
cautus horrescis, nimium premendo
  litus iniquum.

auream quisquis mediocritatem
diligit, tutus caret obsoleti
sordibus tecti, caret invidenda
  sobrius aula.

saevius ventis agitatur ingens
pinus et celsae graviore casu
decidunt turres feriuntque summos
  fulgura montis.

sperat infestis, metuit secundis
alteram sortem bene praeparatum
pectus. informis hiemes reducit
  Iuppiter, idem

summovet. non, si male nunc, et olim
sic erit: quondam cithara tacentem
suscitat Musam neque semper arcum
  tendit Apollo.

rebus angustis animosus atque
fortis appare; sapienter idem
contrahes vento nimium secundo
  turgida vela.

The difference between 1. 38 and 2. 9 is that 1. 38 works superbly as a poem taken to mean what it says, but if we take 2. 9 to mean that Horace is telling Valgius to stop mourning his beloved, and write a panegyric of Augustus instead, it is crass, insensitive, nauseating, and therefore we are wrong. If on the other hand we, on this occasion, assume that Horace's message is about Valgius' poetic work, the poem is well up to the standards we expect from this author.

X

You will take a straighter course, Licinius,
if you are not always thrusting over the deep sea,
or cautiously hugging the dangerous shore too close,
  shivering at the prospect of squalls.

Whoever loves the Golden Mean
is safe (no squalor for him in some shabby old hovel),
and temperate (for him no mansion
  for men to envy).

The huge pine is more cruelly tossed
by the winds, tallest towers
have the heaviest fall, and the lightning flash
  strikes the highest mountains.

The well-prepared heart hopes in adversity
for a change in fortune, and fears it in prosperity.
Jupiter brings back ugly winters
  and Jupiter

removes them. If all goes badly now, some day
it will not be so. Sometimes Apollo rouses
the silent Muse with his lyre. He does not always
  stretch his bow.

In difficult straits, show spirit
and courage, and when the wind
is too strong at your back, be wise
  and shorten the bulging sail.

Odes 2.10

It is no easy matter to make a string of nine moral precepts into a poem, particularly if they are recommending moderation. Horace succeeds, first of all by addressing Licinius. This appears to have been Licinius Murena, brother or half-brother of Maecenas' wife Terentia, and therefore closely connected with Augustus. According to Cassius Dio, 54. 3, when Augustus in 22 BC appeared at a trial and gave evidence for the prosecution, Murena, as defence counsel, asked him what right he had to intervene, 'What are you doing here, and who sent for you?' This was dangerous talk, and sure enough, in that same year Murena was convicted of treason for joining a conspiracy against Augustus and put to death (Crook, 84). Dio says that Murena 'was rough-tongued and headstrong in his manner of speech to everyone'. This poem, and in particular its first and last stanzas, are therefore not airy generalities. They touch upon a matter of life and death as a warning to Licinius Murena, and also as public notification that such warnings are needed. It is as though Horace, friend and patron of Maecenas, knew that Maecenas' brother-in-law was in danger of incurring the displeasure of Augustus, and, as Augustus' poet, is letting it be known where his loyalties lie. This is not moralizing in a vacuum. It is real life, and these are delicate utterances on a dangerous subject. On a careful reading, then, the poem is not, after all, a string of nine moral precepts recommending moderation. At one level it is public advice to Licinius Murena; at another it is a definition of Horace's own view of a contemporary political situation; at another it is his way of dealing with a situation which must have posed a problem in the relationship between Maecenas and Augustus.

The first stanza advises Licinius not always to be bold, and not to be over-cautious. Given what we know about Licinius Murena, the emphasis must lie on the first part of this antithesis. Horace does not pass an explicit judgement, but the implication is clear. The second stanza states a general rule—moderation leads neither to excessive wealth nor to squalid poverty. This carries no discernible reference to Licinius, but the elaboration of this rule in the next stanza leaves no doubt. It forsakes the balanced formulation and points clearly to such as Licinius by noting that it is the great who suffer the worst disasters.

At this midpoint the angle changes as Horace asserts that it is wise to hope in adversity and fear in prosperity. This new point is also understandable in the light of our assumption that Licinius has incurred the displeasure of Augustus, and again it is the first option which is relevant. In adversity, argues Horace, the wise man will hope for a change in fortune. The grounds for such hope are now given in three short clauses pointing out that storm is followed by calm, that bad times are followed by good, and that gods give joy as well as death. Crudely, Licinius is being advised to be patient and wait for a change in his circumstances, but this bland and humdrum advice is couched in terms which take the focus away from a matter of personal prudence to a view of the laws of the universe. The first and third of these clauses accordingly refer to the operations of the gods Jupiter and Apollo. The central argument is expressed in the plainest and weightiest language—'not, if badly now, will it always be thus in time to come'.

The poem ends, as it began, with a nautical image, but this nautical image carries a different injunction, not to steer between constant boldness and over-caution as in the first stanza, but to show courage in adversity, and wise restraint in prosperity. This is an unexceptionable truism, uttered in absolute terms from a point apparently far above any particular circumstances. But, if the above account of Licinius is anywhere near the truth, the thrust is clear, and again it is the first option that speaks to Licinius. He is being advised not to be foolhardy but to exercise self-restraint. The message is that he is in danger of punishment if he does not behave prudently, and that if the occasion should arise, Augustus would be justified in inflicting it. This, of course, is too brutal and obvious for Horace. Nevertheless in 23 BC Licinius, and others, would have known what was meant, and their interpretation would have been confirmed by the events of 22 BC.

Much of the vital energy of the poem comes from its imagery. The first two words, *rectius vives*, mean 'you will live more rightly'; but *rectius*, taken literally, refers to straightness and chimes with the navigational context. The translator can choose to undertranslate, for example with Shepherd, 'The proper course in life' or to overtranslate, as above, 'You will take a straighter course', in order to highlight the metaphor, and at the same time cause some unease. If you take to the deep water, you will in fact be steering a straighter course than if you coast. Horace is playing with a paradox—'You will take the straight course in life if sometimes you do not always take the straight course across the open sea.'

The Golden Mean of the second stanza refers concisely to Aristotle's view that excellence lies between two extremes. But although the thought is common in antiquity, this formulation is first attested here. The phrase is so familiar that we may not see how perverse and daring it is. This is another paradox. What is golden is rare and precious, excellent above all things, the very opposite of what is *mediocris*. So, according to Horace, the Golden Mean is drab, but infinitely precious.

In lines 6–8 wealth and poverty are expressed not as abstracts, but in terms of the homes of the rich and poor, images imprinted on the retinas of the Romans of Horace's day as they walked about their city, and used forcibly by Horace elsewhere, for example at 2. 16. 9–12, and throughout 2. 18.

To us the third stanza may seem to be a trio of tired analogies but Italians would have visualized the umbrella or stone pine, as described on 2. 3. 9, with its globose crown of radiating branches, eminently tossable in strong winds. Romans would have been familiar with fallen buildings in a city of jerry-built tenements, vividly described by Juvenal, 3. 190–6, and the immediacy of the visualization is maintained as Horace imagines the highest mountains struck by flashes of lightning. To us this is trite, but electrical storms in Italy are awesome sights, and would have seemed even more awesome in earlier ages.

Horace seems to be remembering the thought from Lucretius, 5. 1125–6, where envy strikes ambitious men and casts them down like a thunderbolt, from the heights into the terrors of Tartarus:

> e summo, quasi fulmen, deicit ictos
> invidia interdum contemptim in Tartara taetra.

Seneca, in his turn appreciated the power of this image in his *Agamemnon* 96, where 'lightning strikes the lofty hills', *feriunt celsos fulmina colles*, and it is no doubt by way of Seneca that the thought arrives to Thomas Kyd in *The Spanish Tragedy* III. i. 1–4:

> Infortunate condition of kings,
> seated amidst so many helpless doubts!
> First we are plac'd upon extremest height,
> and oft supplanted with exceeding heat.

The standard English edition by Edwards notes that the first eleven lines of this scene are an adaptation of Seneca, *Agamemnon* 57–73, but English scholars have misunderstood the 'heat' of line 4. According to Edwards's commentary 'All edd. read *hate* but the reading has no authority and there is not the slightest reason for suspecting that *heat* is wrong: the meaning of passion, anger, or fury is regular and common.' This is right up to a point, but Seneca, *Agamemnon* 96 quoted above shows that the heat is the lightning which strikes the great. The 'extremest height' is the *celsos colles* of Seneca, helped by the *summos montes* of Horace, *Odes* 2. 12, and 'supplanted' is used in its archaic sense of 'cast down', as in the *Oxford English Dictionary*, s.v. 2.

The second half of the poem begins with an aphorism on hope and fear expressed without metaphor. The grounds for accepting this aphorism are the return and removal of storms (or winters, *hiemes*) by Jupiter, naturally enough since they would fall within the power of the sky-god. In line 15 when he returns them, *hiemes reducit*, the implication is that it was Jupiter who brought them in the first place. This hint thus alludes lightly to the endless cycle of the years and broadens the view of the poem. Apollo the lyre-player was not for the Romans of Augustus' day purely a disembodied intellectual concept. There he stood with his lyre in the precinct of the great temple of Apollo, part of the house of Augustus on the Palatine, and again in the cella inside the temple. Horace plays with our imagination as he presents Apollo as the master of two very different stringed instruments, but there is nothing playful about the final picture of Apollo as the bringer of death, as Licinius was soon to discover.

By a familiar ring composition the final maxim in the poem, like the first, is couched in nautical terms. There is no difficulty about the second limb of it. When there is a strong following wind it is obviously wise to shorten sail, or even to roll the sails on the yardarms and take them down completely; but the first limb is awkward. The rhetorical opposite of shortening sail in a following wind would be to put on full sail in an opposing wind, but this is nonsense. Perhaps this is why Horace does not express that first limb of the precept in metaphorical terms, but quite literally, 'When things are difficult, show bravery and spirit.' But is it quite literal? Nisbet and Hubbard catch a whiff of wind in *animosis*, 'spirited' perhaps suggesting *anima*, 'breeze', and *rebus angustis*, literally 'in narrow circumstances' may support this interpretation. The nautical image is not totally inert, but the ship is in a narrow strait, or perhaps the canvas is shortened, tightened, to tack into head winds. Horace seems to be toying with these possibilities, as he toyed with the sense of *rectius* in the first line of the poem. The image is simple—'ethical choices are like steering a course at sea'—but Horace has a way of throwing extras into the pans of the balance to disturb the equation and provoke the imagination.

Formally, too, he has differentiated between what I have called these nine precepts. The first is a statement in the future tense in the form of a doublet, 'neither . . . nor' filling a stanza. The second stanza is the general statement in the present tense that the Golden Mean is exempt from wealth and poverty. The third is a triad, and the architecture of the three elements is varied in ways which give drama to the Latin and defeat the translator—crudely: 'is waved the huge pine, lofty fall towers, strike highest lightnings mountains'. After these three self-contained stanzas, the theme of the poem changes and so does the pace. Lines 13–20 consist of four propositions, each of which overruns a line, and even the two stanzas are run together. The first of these, the precept, is expressed in literal terms, and the second of the three reasons for it, in lines 17–18, hammers out the fundamental truth in the barest possible literal language. The poem now ends as it began, with a self-contained stanza containing a nautical metaphor and a doublet, stressing the danger of excess by the echo of the word *nimium* from line 3, *nimium premendo* recalled by *nimium secundo*. This dry analysis is for the brain, but for the listener it is part of the drama of the poem, leaving, as it ends, the sound of danger ringing in the ears of Licinius. Even the syntax reinforces the music. The poem consists of general statements in every stanza except the first and the last. These are addressed to Licinius and the last is a command. Licinius is in danger.

Typical of Horace, too, are the internal links. For example, the high sea, *altum*, of the first line, looks forward to the three heights in the third stanza, the squalls of line 2 to the storms of lines 9 and 15. The architec-

---

XI

Quid bellicosus Cantaber et Scythes,
Hirpine Quincti, cogitet Hadria
divisus obiecto, remittas
quaerere, nec trepides in usum

poscentis aevi pauca: fugit retro
levis iuventas et decor, arida
pellente lascivos amores
canitie facilemque somnum.

non semper idem floribus est honor
vernis, neque uno Luna rubens nitet
vultu: quid aeternis minorem
consiliis animum fatigas?

cur non sub alta vel platano vel hac
pinu iacentes sic temere et rosa
canos odorati capillos,
dum licet, Assyriaque nardo

tural image of the second stanza speaks to the high towers of lines 10–11. The dangers of the sea are contrasted with the safety expressed by *tutus* in line 6. The lightning flashes of line 12, echoes of Lucretius on envy at 5. 1125–6 as just quoted, lead our mind back to the envy excited by wealth in lines 7–8.

But the power of the poem depends also on the fact that the general view it presents is not the mouthing of stock philosophical commonplaces, and not merely a statement of loyalty from a client poet in a particular political situation, but a vital part of the world view which Horace has arrived at and which he presents repeatedly with such conviction in his poetry. Not for him the extremes of sexual desire or gluttony. Not for him the lust for power or wealth. Although the *Weltanschauung* is commonplace, it has some interest because it is Horace who is recommending it. There can be no doubt that he was an extremist in his love of country life, his enjoyment of his friends, his occasional convivial excesses, his devotion to Greek literature, his dedication to the Muse, and the lifetime of hard work which that entailed.

XI

Do not trouble to ask, Quinctius, my Hirpanian friend,
what the war-loving Cantabrian is thinking, or the Scythian
—he's kept well away by the barrier of the Adriatic—
and stop worrying about what you need in life.

Life asks so little. Smooth-faced youth
and beauty turn and run
and dry grey hair puts love's pleasures
and easy sleep to flight.

The glory of spring flowers does not last
for ever. The blushing moon does not always shine
with the same face. Why weary your little mind
with eternal thoughts?

Why do we not lie down under a tall plane tree,
or here without more ado under this pine,
and drink, while we may, our grey heads
perfumed with the rose and anointed

potamus uncti? dissipat Euhius
curas edaces. quis puer ocius
restinguet ardentis Falerni
pocula praetereunte lympha?

quis devium scortum eliciet domo
Lyden? eburna dic age cum lyra
maturet incomptum Lacaenae
more comas religata nodum.

This is a poem in two halves, the first telling Quinctius what not to do, the second telling him what to do. He is not to think about hostile peoples at the western and north-eastern limits of the world, not to worry about the necessities of life (lines 4–5 mean literally: 'the needs of time which demands few things'), and not to exhaust his mind with problems of eternity, for which it is too small, *minorem*. In the second half, he is urged to lie down under a tree and enjoy wine, music, and love. These are the usual platitudes. How does Horace give them poetic life?

First, this is *ad hominem* poetry, spoken to a particular man in a particular situation. When Horace asks why they do not lie down under a plane tree 'or here without more ado under this pine', we are being asked to visualize the two men walking in Quinctius' park. So Quinctius is rich—the expensive unguent and Falernian of 16–18 confirm this—and his temperament is such that Horace can present him as a man inclined to worry. The *mis-en-scène* is familiar to us from *Odes* 2. 3, and here the two men are on such close terms that Horace can suggest a drinking party on his friend's estate, telling him what his slaves ought to be doing and what woman Quinctius should be inviting. This is a poem of friendship.

Little else can be said with certainty about Quinctius. Until 1978 it had always been assumed that his name was Quinctius Hirpinus. In that year, however, Nisbet and Hubbard reported in their commentary that in about 85 BC a Gaius Quinctius had been a patron of the Hirpini, a warlike people who lived in the southern Apennines. This leads us into the humour of the poem. If Hirpinus is not a personal name but an indication of the home of Quinctius' family, then Horace is amusingly suggesting that this wealthy Roman sophisticate is a tough backwoodsman from the mountains of central Italy. Such a Samnite would clearly not be worrying about the bellicosity of Cantabrians, and high in his strongholds in the Apennines he would not be anxious as he looked north-east and imagined the Adriatic Sea (and all the vast tracts of land) which lay between him and Scythia.

with Assyrian nard? Euhius dispels
all gnawing cares. Won't some boy come quick
and douse the fire of the Falernian
from the stream flowing by?

Won't someone tempt Lyde
from her secluded home? Go on, tell her to hurry
and take her ivory lyre, tying her hair up uncombed
in a knot in the Spartan style.

Now that Quinctius has been gently chided for anxieties about the security of Rome's frontiers, Horace alludes to philosophy. Lines 5–6 are sound Epicureanism. Horace loved Lucretius, for example, and would have remembered *ad victum quae flagitat usus, omnia iam ferme mortalibus esse parata*, 'Almost everything which need demands for their sustenance, is already provided for mortals' (*De Rerum Natura* 6. 9–10). So Quinctius is buttressed against poverty not only by the fact that he owns so much, but also by the Epicurean truth that life asks for so little. His next anxiety is also philosophical. Among eternal problems in Latin poetry meteorological phenomena bulk large. 'Le silence éternel de ces espaces infinis' (Pascal, *Pensées* 3. 206), was a constant subject for speculation and trepidation in antiquity. This way of thinking is condemned by Epicurus and derided by Lucretius as, for example, in Epicurus, *Principal Doctrine* 13, 'There is no advantage in acquiring safety with reference to men, if suspicions remain about what is beneath and what is above the earth, and indeed what is in the infinite universe.' In *Epistles* 1. 12. 18 Horace himself asks mockingly 'what conceals the dark orb of the moon, and what reveals it'. In a passage which Horace knew (see *Odes* 4. 7. 7–13), Lucretius, 5. 732–50 had already given an answer to that question (West 1994*b*: 18–19). *Epistles* 1. 16 is also addressed to a Quinctius, and it, too, has a philosophical element, Stoic, not Epicurean in tone. If the two poems are addressed to the same Quinctius, it is possible that he was a serious-minded person whom Horace in the ode is advising to be less serious and to enjoy the advantages he possesses.

So far the poem is enriched, as so often, by tension between opposites (see West 1973), between the Hirpini and foreign peoples, and between anxiety and freedom from it in lines 3–4. The second stanza has more of these tensions. In old age the hair is grey and dry, so when it is in contrast with the smoothness of youth, we are bound to think not only of youthful skin, but also of the glossy sheen of black Italian hair. Beauty and youth are in retreat and grey hair is driving away their pleasures. In the next stanza the vastness of eternity is contrasted with the human mind. There may even be a hidden contrast in the reference to the moon. If the blushing moon does not always shine with the same face, surely that refers not only to the phases of the moon but also carries with it the thought that the moon is not always tinged with red.

Contrasts and hints of contrasts continue in the second half of the poem. The plane tree is high and we should lie under it. Let us strew roses, canonically red, in our grey hair. Cares are nibbling at us but Euhius, that is Bacchus the god of wine, drives them away. In line 19 there are, literally, cups of burning Falernian wine and a slave boy must come and extinguish them with water. Lyde is no lady of the street, but lives in her own secluded house, from which she must be lured.

It would be wrong to see these contrasts as a handy mechanism for producing ornamental epithets. This is a superficial and unworthy suggestion. Each of the above terms taken singly would be interesting enough—Falernian could no doubt be an ardent wine, and Lyde was so prosperous that she could afford to live in a secluded area of Rome, but set beside them a boy running for water to cool down the wine and another rushing to tempt Lyde from her home and readers are immediately receiving impressions and stimuli which involve them in speculations and make reading an active and absorbing experience. This is Horace's poetic logic in action. The contrasts are lightly touched upon. Readers find themselves working out details, and implications.

This activity is not confined to single sentences. Some of the poetic vitality may arise from a contrast in the broad argument of the poem. In 1. 17, for example, there is a complex interplay between the rural scene of the first part and the human scene in the second. Here, in 2. 11, the clash is between what Quinctius should not worry about and what he should. The fears of the opening of the first half are a far cry from the drinking scene which begins the second. The grey hair of line 7 is now to be sleek with spikenard and fragrant with roses, which in turn speak back to the short-lived flowers of spring of line 9. The possibility of a simple, modest way of life in line 5 is not at all like the luxuries which Horace now recommends. In line 7 old age is driving love away, but the poem ends with measures to persuade Lyde to come.

But the vital wit of the poem consists of the paradox that the pleasures recommended in its second half require the strenuousness which Horace has forbidden in its first. Quinctius has been urged to relax, not to worry, and not to weary his mind but now in the second half there is no time to lose. Enjoyment calls for immediate and vigorous action. 'Let us lie down under this tall plane tree, or here, just as we are (*sic temere*) under this pine.' And 'let us strew roses in our hair while we may (*dum licet*)'. Bacchus himself scatters cares, and *dissipat* is a violent word, as well as a humorous one—he specializes in other forms of dissipation. A slave boy is needed rather quickly, *ocius*, to put out a fire. The stream is passing, and Lyde must be told to hurry, *maturet*, and not bother with an elaborate hair-do. Quinctius is being told to relax, and be quick about it, before age drives away his youth.

Critics of Horace have found this ode a string of clichés. Perhaps a way of demonstrating that it is something different is to contrast it with the similar fragment of Greek poetry cited by Nisbet and Hubbard which might be translated as follows, only a little too cheerfully and with two additions to produce rhymes suggesting the jingle of the Anacreontic metre:

Upon this smooth-leaved myrtle
on the lotus-fragrant grass
I want to drink in comfort
[and hear the river pass].
Why labour in the quarry?
Why sow the land with seed?
Put scent and roses on my hair
a woman's what I need.
Before I leave this earthly life
and join the dance below,
I'll drive away my worries
[that's one thing that I know].

(*Anacreontea* 30)

XII

Nolis longa ferae bella Numantiae
nec durum Hannibalem nec Siculum mare
Poeno purpureum sanguine mollibus
  aptari citharae modis,

nec saevos Lapithas et nimium mero
Hylaeum domitosque Herculea manu
Telluris iuvenes, unde periculum
  fulgens contremuit domus

Saturni veteris; tuque pedestribus
dices historiis proelia Caesaris,
Maecenas, melius ductaque per vias
  regum colla minacium.

me dulces dominae Musa Licymniae
cantus, me voluit dicere lucidum
fulgentis oculos et bene mutuis
  fidum pectus amoribus,

quam nec ferre pedem dedecuit choris
nec certare ioco nec dare bracchia
ludentem nitidis virginibus sacro
  Dianae celebris die.

num tu quae tenuit dives Achaemenes
aut pinguis Phrygiae Mygdonias opes
permutare velis crine Licymniae,
  plenas aut Arabum domos,

cum flagrantia detorquet ad oscula
cervicem aut facili saevitia negat,
quae poscente magis gaudeat eripi,
  interdum rapere occupet?

Callimachus, Greek poet and scholar at the court of the Ptolemies in Alexandria in the middle of the 3rd century BC, had a profound influence on Latin poets of the Augustan era. Amongst the hallmarks of his style are brevity and the avoidance of bombast, as expounded in his *Aetia*, witty and learned elegies on the origins of Greek customs and institutions:

XII

Long wars in fierce Numantia, Hannibal iron-hard,
the Sicilian sea purpled with Punic blood—
you would not wish these themes set
  to the soft measures of the lyre,

nor savage Lapiths, nor Hylaeus ungovernable
in his cups, nor the defeat at the hand of Hercules
of the warrior sons of earth, whose threats
  shook the gleaming house

of old Saturn; and you will do better yourself, Maecenas,
by speaking in prose histories of Caesar's battles
and menacing kings dragged through the streets
  by their necks.

As for me, the Muse has wished that I should speak
of the sweet songs of the lady Licymnia, of her eyes
brightly shining, and her heart truly faithful
  to a requited love.

She was not disgraced in chorus of dancers
or contest of wit, or playing arm in arm
with shining maidens in crowded temple
  on Diana's holy day.

Surely you would not wish to exchange all the possessions
of Achaemenes, or the wealth of Mygdon
in fat Phrygia, or the full-stocked homes of the Arabs,
  for a strand of Licymnia's hair

when she bends down her neck to burning kisses,
or cruelly teases by refusing them, though she enjoys
stolen kisses more than the one who asks for them,
  and sometimes is quick to steal them herself.

Mine not to thunder; that is Zeus's job.
When first I laid my writing tablet on my knees,
  Apollo, god of Lycia, spoke to me:
'Dear poet,' he said, 'do keep your sacrifices fat,
  but give me, please, a nice slim Muse.'

. . . .

> Let others bray and bluster like the long-eared beast
> I would be light and winged.
>
> (*Aetia*, fragments 1. 20–4, 31–2)

Roman poets took over this statement of poetic intent, using it frequently as a *recusatio*, a polite refusal to write lengthy epics in praise of Roman military achievements (see Lyne 1995: 30–9). Standard features of the *recusatio* are:

1. the intervention of a god, often Apollo or the Muse;
2. the refusal to write long mythological epics or to praise the military achievements of the addressee;
3. the grounds for the refusal, usually the poet's incompetence, his own talents being too slight for such high tasks;
4. the suggestion of some more suitable poet.

Under the first head the poet can claim divine sanction for his decision; under the second he can briefly praise the addressee while declining to do so, thus avoiding the appearance of flattery, and he can also demonstrate competence in the style which he is pretending to be beyond him; in the third he can briefly show his skills in his own chosen field; in the fourth he can compliment a fellow poet in addition to the addressee, thus economically praising two persons in one poem. These are the basic, obvious advantages of this framework. Horace's use of it is always more subtle, or witty, or intense. Such an adaptation of the form has already appeared in this book (2. 9).

Looking at these four categories as they appear in 2. 12, we see that the wishes of the Muse are not consulted until the fourth stanza. On the other hand, the first word of the Latin is *nolis*, 'You would not wish'. Horace has wittily cast Maecenas in the role of the intervening power. This gambit enables him adroitly to conform to the second of the above categories. He does not *refuse* to write of the military achievements of Augustus, but rather lays the responsibility for his decision upon Maecenas. He covers the third category by stressing the unsuitability of his lyre in line 4, by deferring to the will of the Muse in line 13, and by proceeding to show his paces as a writer of poetry about love in the rest of the ode. In the third stanza he has covered the fourth of the categories not by putting forward the name of a more competent poet, but by suggesting that the campaigns of Augustus will be better described by Maecenas himself in prose.

Although he has adroitly postponed the name of Caesar Augustus, as soon as we reach the end of the grand sentence which finishes at line 12 we realize that Augustus has been on the scene from the beginning. Numantia, a city in northern central Spain near the headwaters of the river Douro, had been captured after bitter resistance which lasted from 195 until its destruction in 133 BC (see *Oxford Classical Dictionary* (1996) under 'Numantia') but Horace's first readers would have thought of the fierce war Augustus fought in 26–25 BC against the Cantabri, the northern neighbours of Numantia. Horace then moves back in time by way of Hannibal and the Second Punic War in 218–201 BC to the great sea battles of the First Punic War, when Rome defeated the Carthaginians at Mylae (260 BC), and the Aegates Islands (241 BC) off the western tip of Sicily. But no Roman could read of the Sicilian sea purpled with blood without thinking of the battles fought in Sicilian waters by Octavian and Agrippa against Sextus Pompeius, including Agrippa's victory in a second battle of Mylae in 36 BC. Maecenas, to whom this ode is addressed, having been an eyewitness, would surely have remembered them well (Cassius Dio, 48. 47–8 and Appian, 5. 84–90). The journey back in time continues into mythology with the story of the drunken brawl between the Lapiths and Centaurs (Hylaeus was a Centaur) at the wedding of Pelops and Hippodamia, and comes to its grand climax and its earliest date with the attempt of the Giants to scale Olympus. After the Augustan undertones in the first stanza, we should remember that Horace uses this episode as an allegory for Octavian's war against Antony and Cleopatra at 1. 3. 40, 3. 1. 7, and 3. 4. 49–80. Horace has declined to praise Augustus, but has praised him. He has declined to celebrate his battles, but has evoked them. In this context it may even be that the two instances of drunkenness in lines 5–6 are an echo of the drunkenness of Antony (see *Odes* 1. 37. 12–14), which had been such a salient feature of Octavian's propaganda war that Antony had written a pamphlet in his own defence, *De Ebrietate Sua*.

In 1. 6 Horace insisted upon his own inability to write epic, but instead of seizing the opportunity to display his epic powers, he proved the point by making a botch of the epic style, referring to the anger of Achilles as the bad temper of the son of Peleus, and to Odysseus the man of many resources as Odysseus the double-dealer. Here, however, in 2. 12 the emphasis lies not on his incapacity, but rather on the assertion that war poetry does not go easily with the lyre. He now shows that he can rise to the epic style, notably by the high art of the long first sentence. The adjectives are ordinary words but in this context not inert. The Numantine War was *long*, more than sixty years, and the Numantines were *fierce* under siege and in defeat, resorting even to cannibalism and mass suicide. Hannibal was a *tough* enemy, ranging over Italian soil between 218 and 207 BC and inflicting unforgettable defeats on Roman armies at Trebia, Trasimene, and Cannae. The translation fails. The Latin calls Hannibal *durum* 'hard', but that bare word does not sound like English in this context. Nevertheless it has to be preserved in some form because the vitality of the poetry depends on the vigorous tension between these first three adjectives and the soft, *mollibus*, strains of the lyre in line 4. Unlike the wars, which were long, fierce, and hard, the poems of Horace will be short, gentle, and soft.

Another bold effect in this opening is the purpling of the Sicilian sea with blood. In an impassioned condemnation of contemporary decadence at *Odes* 3. 6. 33–4 we read 'parents like these did not produce the young warriors who stained the sea with Carthaginian blood':

> non his iuventus orta parentibus
> infecit aequor sanguine Punico.

This lofty sentiment is heightened by a word play which is even clearer here in 2. 12. The Carthaginians are colonists from Tyre in Phoenicia, and reddish-purple dye, extracted from the shellfish *murex*, was exported from Tyre and known as Tyrian or Phoenician purple. The adjective *phoenicius*, *puniceus*, means either Phoenician or purple, and the pun is already used by Plautus in *Pseudolus* where the brothel-keeper, threatening to whip his girls, turns to Phoenicium and says that he will present her with a purple hide, *Phoenicium poeniceo corio* (line 230). (In Latin -ph- is pronounced not -f-, but -p- + an aspirate.) Etymological play is not only comic. It is also at home in the epic style, as for example in Virgil (see O'Hara).

Not only does Horace ring the changes on the refusal to praise, but he also plays games with the fourth standard feature listed above, the recommendation of a substitute. We are invited to believe that Maecenas has suggested to Horace that he should write poetry in praise of Augustus' battles, and Horace's reply is that the patron would be better at doing this than the poet. It is by no means easy to gauge the tone of this. On the face of it there is nothing absurd about the suggestion. It seems that Maecenas had fought at Octavian's side in several campaigns, at Mutina in 42 BC, in the war against Sextus Pompeius, and at the battle of Actium (*Epodes* 1 and 9), and could have produced a vivid eyewitness account like Asinius Pollio's as referred to in *Odes* 2. 1. Maecenas, too, was a writer. On the other hand, what we know of his writing in prose and verse (see Norden: 292–4) and the discussion below of *Odes* 2. 17) suggests that it was mannered and self-conscious. It is not easy to imagine Maecenas as a military historian. These two men (and Augustus) wrote to each other in robust and teasing terms and the pun at *pedestribus historiis* in line 10 makes it likely that the recommendation of Maecenas as a panegyrist is also a tease: the adjective is often applied to infantry troops. The historian is the foot-soldier of literature.

This poem raises an ancient, unsolved problem. Is Licymnia Horace's mistress or Maecenas' wife? The translation offered above for line 14 comes down on one side of this controversy. The translation of *dominae Licymniae* as 'the lady Licymnia' suggests that she is the mistress of the house, like Proserpina the wife of the god of the Underworld, *dominam Ditis*, at Virgil, *Aeneid* 6. 397, like Barine at *Odes* 2. 8. 19, and Circe at *Epistles* 1. 2. 25 (*pace* Davis 1975: 72). This is what the word always means in Horace. But since in Roman elegy the *domina* is often the 'mistress' in an erotic sense, most recent scholars (Morris and Williams, Lyne 1995: 104) would prefer to understand the phrase as referring not to Maecenas' wife, but to Horace's mistress, taking line 21 to mean 'surely [if you were in my shoes] you would not wish to give up a strand of her hair'. There are several strong arguments in favour of this view. First, Maecenas is near the centre of the Augustan circle, and the detailed description of kissing in love-play in the last stanza, unique in the odes, could seem unthinkable applied to the relationship of such a grandee and his wife. Second, according to the *recusatio* formula, in refusing to praise the celebrity the poet may state his intention to praise his own mistress, never the celebrity's wife. Third, the activities of the fifth stanza do not conform to the Roman conception of the proper behaviour for a respectable married woman. A chorus of matrons is unthinkable, a married woman is not praised for competing successfully in jokes or fun or games or amoebean raillery, whatever *certare iocis* may mean, and why did a wife give her arms to shining maidens as she played with them on Diana's holy day?

This is a formidable case and it may be the truth. But the stanza in which Licymnia dances with virgins, difficult as it is for the married woman, is not easy for one of Horace's lovers, be she freedwoman or slave. Witty repartee might well be part of her armoury but would one of the ladies of pleasure who are Horace's lovers have been dancing with shining virgins at the festival of the goddess of virginity? Nor is the argument from the expectations of the *recusatio* totally convincing. We have seen Horace's taste for surprise in this poem and it could be documented scores of times that he is no slave to formulae. On the contrary, steeped as he is in the Greek and Latin poetic tradition, he bends that tradition again and again to his own will. The author of a *recusatio* who tells his patron to do the job himself is well capable of taking delight in cheating our expectations by ending with his patron's wife instead of his own mistress. It may also be noticed that Horace's allusions to his own lovers at this point in other examples of the *recusatio* formula are always brief and modest. If these two stanzas are praise of Horace's mistress, they are not in Horace's usual style.

The decision comes down to the propriety of the final stanza. In assessing that, we have to assess Maecenas. The third *Epode* ends with a warning that if Maecenas ever serves a dish with too much garlic in it, Horace will pray that Maecenas' mistress will put up her hand against his kiss and lie away from him in bed. At *Epodes* 14. 13 Maecenas is passionately in love and the context suggests that the object of his affections is a mime dancer, Bathyllus (Lyne 1995: 103). In themselves these passages prove nothing about Maecenas. Epodes are required to be scurrilous. They are not historical documents, and they are very different from odes. On the other hand they do demonstrate that Horace could go quite far in teasing Maecenas publicly in his writings. This general point is borne out by surviving letters from Augustus which demonstrate that coarse badinage was common coin between these three men. It was Augustus writing to Horace, who joked about his paunch, *ventriculus*, and called him 'the purest possible penis' *purissimum penem*, and 'the sweetest little mannikin', *homuncionem lepidissimum* (Suetonius, *Life of Horace*). Similarly Augustus, in a letter to Maecenas, ends a list of ten pleasantly abusive terms by calling his friend a *malagma moecharum*, where the Greek word *malagma* refers to padding, and therefore the phrase might be translated as 'adulteresses' duvet' (Macrobius, 2. 4. 12).

What sort of man was this Maecenas? He was born around 70 BC, and for a dozen years after the assassination of Julius Caesar in 44 BC he fought alongside Octavian, who used his talents in a series of delicate and important negotiations. From 36 to 29 BC, alone or with Agrippa, he often represented Octavian in Rome, exercising full powers, which he used in 30 BC, for example, to detect the conspiracy of Lepidus and execute him. During this time he was charged with the task of opening all Octavian's official letters, and given a duplicate of his seal so that he could rephrase them to suit the situation, and could also issue such edicts and letters as he judged circumstances to require (Pliny, *Natural History* 37. 10, Dio, 51. 3). Augustus, a sound judge of such matters, found him an active administrator, a tactful and brilliant negotiator, and utterly reliable. He was seven years older than Octavian and it seems that he was a trusted adviser, and on occasion restrained the violence of the younger man. Propertius was right in saying, 'the true monument to Maecenas will be his loyalty', *Maecenatis erunt vera tropaea fides*, 3. 9. 34). Even Seneca, who despised him, knew that this was a noble and manly character, *ingenium grande et virile* (*Epistles* 92. 35).

Maecenas had another side to his character. Lyne observes that he was 'notorious for his foppish and affected prose' (Lyne 1995: 105). These terms are derived from the few surviving fragments of his works (see notes on *Odes* 2. 17) and ancient comments. Augustus teased him for the preciosity of his language (Macrobius, 2. 4. 12) and Seneca in *Epistles* 114 uses him as an example of how an indisciplined style is the mark of a loose-living man. He came from noble and wealthy Etruscan stock. His father was a Roman knight, *eques*, a rank which required a high property qualification, and he seems to have preserved the traditional Etruscan belief in the importance of enjoying life. He built himself a palace on the Esquiline Hill in Rome with glorious gardens and the famous tower from which Nero was later to watch Rome burning while singing his poem on the taking of Troy. If Horace's poems are to be believed, Maecenas had a gift for convivial friendship. He was a lover of Greek literature and himself wrote dialogues and satires (West, 1995*b*), the latter in a mixture of prose and verse. Some examples are quoted in the comments on 2. 17, but his greatest achievement was as a patron of poets. By his support for Horace and Virgil he has put many hundreds of thousands of people in his debt, and perhaps that debt will continue to accrue. He remained an *eques*, although he could have been elevated to senatorial rank and, even when he was in effect governing Rome and Italy, he attended to official business wearing informal clothes and walked round the city with an escort of two eunuchs. He doted on his wife, so much so that according to Seneca's sneer in *Epistles* 114, he married her a thousand times.

In piecing together these fragments of information and of gossip, we begin to suspect that Maecenas was his own man, happy to do what he thought fit and not worry about public opinion. Woodman (1983: 239–44) suggests that the unbuttoned style of the man may even have conveyed a political message to the effect that Augustus had nothing to fear from any personal ambition in that quarter. The end of this ode certainly breaches what we now call the generic conventions, but in Maecenas and Horace we are dealing with men of enormous ability, a taste for innovation, and a willingness to flout accepted standards and thwart the expectations of their readers.

The date of composition of the ode is unknown, but Maecenas may have married some time before 30 BC (see Nisbet and Hubbard 1978:

182). It is surely possible that Horace is cheerfully referring to his patron's notorious love for his wife. This might ease the difficulties of lines 17–20. This stanza could be reminding Maecenas of how beautiful she looked and how well she performed when *before her marriage* she joined in the joyous dances on the holy day of the virgin goddess Diana, laughing and linking arms with the other virgins. There is another possibility worth considering. The Roman poets we know of this era are not numerous, and they often refer to each other's works, as we have already seen in *Odes* 1. 24, 2. 6, and 2. 9. Catullus, for instance, alludes in *Poems* 96 to the love poems Calvus addressed to his beloved Quintilia. Now Maecenas wrote of love, as we know from the typical fragment which might be translated in some such way as this: 'he curls his face into a grimace for the woman, and bills at her with his lips, sighing as he begins, like the tyrants of the woods debasing themselves by bending their weary neck', *feminae cinno crispat et labris columbatur incipitque suspirans, ut cervice lassa fanantur nemoris tyranni* (*Epistles* 114. 5). The man who wrote this might have written uninhibitedly about his love, and the last stanza of 2. 12 may be a distant allusion to some such thing he wrote.

There is one other scrap of evidence that may support this in the comments preserved in the margins of some manuscripts of Horace, going under the name of pseudo-Acro. These were culled from ancient sources probably in the fifth century AD, and include some useful information not found in earlier sources (see Nisbet and Hubbard 1970: pp. xlix–li). According to pseudo-Acro, Licymnia is a pseudonym for Terentia Licinia, wife of Maecenas, half-sister of the Licinius of *Odes* 2. 10. In the Latin poets there are several examples of such pseudonyms, always syllabically equivalent to the real names. Apuleius, *Apology* 10 lists Lesbia for Clodia, Lycoris for Cytheris, Delia for Plania, Cynthia for Hostia, Perilla for Metella.

This lengthy comment on 2. 12 will end with two small points of translation. Syndikus has pointed out that the same verb, *velle*, occurs at three points in the poem. It opens the poem in its negative form as *nolis*, and it recurs as *voluit* in line 14, and as *velis* in line 23. He goes on to argue that this repetition helps to articulate the logic of the poem—'you would not wish wars to be set to *my* lyre and *you* will tell of them better yourself' (1–12); 'the Muse has wished *me* to tell of Licymnia and *you* would not wish to exchange a strand of her hair' (13–28). It would be doctrinaire to demand that a translation should always keep the same word repeats as the original. Here, for instance, the verb *dicere*, 'to speak' occurs at lines 10 and 14 but does not seem to bear much logical or poetic stress. But if Syndikus is right and the repetition *velle* signposts the logic of the poem, surely the translator must preserve the repetition. It might be a fair test of translations to check whether they do so. None of the first six I have looked at does.

The last stanza of this ode is the most difficult stanza in all the odes for the translator. This is clearly indicated in my own laboured version above and in the following attempt by Shepherd:

> . . . when she bends her neck to your glowing
> kisses, or (gently stubborn) denies you, since
> (more than you wooing) she likes to have them
> stolen, and sometimes she steals first?

This is accurate, but not a pleasure to read. The two parentheses give it a jolting movement and tax the understanding and patience. There is also a mistake. The parenthesis 'gently stubborn' does not capture the force of *facili saevitia*, literally 'easy cruelty'. *Facilis* is a word commonly used to indicate sexual compliance. A woman who is easy is a woman of easy virtue. The sharp contradiction in the phrase, the oxymoron, suggests that Licymnia resists fiercely for a time and then happily consents. 'Gently stubborn' is not very near this.

James Michie is a poet:

> . . . When she bends her neck to your burning mouth? Resist
> Soft-stubbornly she may, but even your thirst
> To kiss is less than hers is to be kissed
> And sometimes she drinks first.

Here the technique is commanding. The forceless overlaps which drag in Shepherd's version have disappeared. The enjambement of 'Resist', on the other hand, is an effective transfer of the effect of the enjambement of *cervicem* in line 26 of the Latin. But the great brilliance lies in the turning of a restriction into a resource. Rhyme narrows down the poet's choice, but here the rhyme of 'thirst' and 'first' brings in a vivid image which has enabled the poet to produce a smooth and elegant version of a complicated action. On the other hand, the scholar might raise his eyebrows at the importation of this thirst and drinking, and would mourn the loss of the picture provided by the word 'down', in the first line and of the crime of theft in the third and fourth. The poetry of Michie is a joy to read, and close to the Latin, but not close enough for a reader who wants to know what Horace has said.

XIII

Ille et nefasto te posuit die
quicumque primum, et sacrilega manu
produxit, arbos, in nepotum
perniciem opprobriumque pagi;

illum et parentis crediderim sui
fregisse cervicem et penetralia
sparsisse nocturno cruore
hospitis; ille venena Colcha

et quidquid usquam concipitur nefas
tractavit, agro qui statuit meo
te triste lignum, te caducum
in domini caput immerentis.

quid quisque vitet numquam homini satis
cautum est in horas: navita Bosphorum
Poenus perhorrescit neque ultra
caeca timet aliunde fata;

miles sagittas et celerem fugam
Parthi, catenas Parthus et Italum
robur; sed improvisa leti
vis rapuit rapietque gentis.

quam paene furvae regna Proserpinae
et iudicantem vidimus Aeacum
sedesque descriptas piorum et
Aeoliis fidibus querentem

Sappho puellis de popularibus,
et te sonantem plenius aureo,
Alcaee, plectro dura navis,
dura fugae mala, dura belli!

utrumque sacro digna silentio
mirantur umbrae dicere; sed magis
pugnas et exactos tyrannos
densum umeris bibit aure vulgus.

XIII

Not only did he plant you on an unholy day,
whoever did it first, but he also tended you
with sacrilegious hand, a tree to destroy
his descendants and disgrace the district,

and I could believe he strangled his own father
and spilt a guest's blood in the dead of night
on the shrine of his household gods.
He dealt in Colchian poisons

and every crime conceived in every corner
of the world—the man who planted you on my land,
you evil timber, set to fall
on your innocent master's head.

No man can ever see for sure from hour to hour
what to avoid. The Phoenician sailor shudders
at the Bosphorus, and, clear of the straits, fails
to see death coming from some other quarter.

The soldier is afraid of arrows and the Parthian's swift flight.
The Parthian fears chains and a Roman dungeon,
but no man foresees the stroke of death which has carried off
the peoples of the earth, and always will.

How nearly did we see the kingdom
of dark Proserpina, and Aeacus in judgement,
and the seats of the holy set apart,
and Sappho complaining

of her young countrywomen to her Aeolian lyre,
and you, Alcaeus, sounding in fuller tones
with your golden plectrum the rigours of shipboard,
the cruel rigours of exile, the rigours of war.

The shades listen in wonderment and sacred silence
to the words of both, but with more willing ear
the crowd packed shoulder to shoulder drinks in
battles and expulsions of tyrants.

quid mirum, ubi illis carminibus stupens
demittit atras belua centiceps
auris et intorti capillis
Eumenidum recreantur angues?

quin et Prometheus et Pelopis parens
dulci laborem decipitur sono,
nec curat Orion leones
aut timidos agitare lyncas.

The first dozen lines are all fun. Horace has almost been killed by a falling tree on his own estate, or so he says. The poem begins by his denunciation, not of the tree, but of the countryman who had planted it. Horace is an intelligent and fair-minded man. This is not only a gross injustice, but also nonsense.

The villainous tree-planter is said to have committed, or to have been capable of committing, six crimes arranged in pairs, with each pair opening with the pronoun, *ille* or *illum*, to raise the rhetorical tone. He is guilty of impiety and sacrilege in lines 1 and 2, then probably, in Horace's view, also of parricide and the murder of a house guest, and certainly of poisoning (by means of the arts of Medea, princess of Colchis), and every impiety that man has ever thought of in every corner of the globe. This is more nonsense. If he actually had committed every impiety ever conceived, then Horace had no need to advance parricide as his own unsupported opinion in line 6. Horace is working himself up into a lather.

Greeks and Romans were interested in the origins of things, and frequently condemned the originators of evil. Horace, for instance, condemns the man who sailed the first ship (*Odes* 1. 3. 10–12). Now, this unknown countryman planted a tree, but he did not plant the first tree, and it is grossly unfair of Horace to use the words *quicumque primum* here and so associate him with these archetypal examples of man's pride and ambition. Those who plant trees are benefactors of posterity. This poor man is accused, quite absurdly, of planting in order to destroy his descendants (notice the plural in line 4).

The overheated language continues in the second stanza. To kill one's father is one thing; to strangle him is another. To kill a guest in your house is a crime against the gods, including the Penates, gods of the house and gods of hospitality, *hospitales dei* in Cicero, *Verrines* 4. 48; to kill him while he sleeps and spatter the *penetralia*, the shrine of the Penates, with his blood, is horror upon horror upon horror. It must be a joke.

Little wonder, when the hundred-headed monster,
struck dumb by this singing, lets down his black ears,
and coiling snakes come to life
in the hair of the Furies.

Even Prometheus and the father of Pelops
are cheated of their labour by the sweet music,
and Orion neglects to drive the lions
and the timorous lynxes.

Part of the fun is that after this character assassination we still do not know whose character is being assassinated. It is not till line 10 that the offender is disclosed, the man who set you up '*you* evil timber on *my* land' and the Latin is all the more pseudo-poignant because the possessive adjectives stand next each other, *meo te*. The curse is an established poetic form and this is a neat variant upon it carried to preposterous lengths of vehemence and injustice. Even before the last heart-rending word, *immerentis*, undeserving, Horace has made sure that we know that this is all cheerful nonsense.

At line 13 the tone suddenly changes. 'No man has ever seen for sure what he should guard against from hour to hour' is a hard fact of human life expressed in simple words. Phoenicians were great seafarers and traders, but even the Phoenician shudders as he sails through the Bosphorus towards the Black Sea. Well he might since the ancients (see Lucretius, 5. 506–8) believed that the Bosphorus always flowed westwards, *fluit rapidus . . . in unam partem semper pronus et torrens* (Seneca, *Naturales Quaestiones* 4. 2. 29) 'swift, headlong and in spate, and in one direction' or to use a livelier version:

> the Pontick sea,
> Whose icy current and compulsive course
> Ne'er feels retiring ebb, but keeps due on
> To the Propontick and the Hellespont.
> (Shakespeare, *Othello* III. iii. 516–19)

On the other hand, once he is past the Bosphorus (*ultra*, 'beyond'), as he sighs with relief in the calmer waters of the Black Sea, death unforeseen strikes him from some other quarter.

The ode started with Horace having fun with an incident in his own life and then moved to a weighty universal law. Now back to Horace. 'How nearly we came to see the kingdom of dark Proserpina'. How serious is this? What is Horace trying to say? In the words of Nisbet and

Hubbard, 'what is the intention of the whole?' Did his narrow escape from the falling tree lead him to see his place in the hierarchy of poets and contemplate the possibility of his own survival after death (Reitzenstein, 358)? Is it likely that 'the frequency with which Horace returned to the incident of the falling tree suggests an abiding concern that resisted all attempts to banish it by ridicule' (Commager, 141)? Was the poem born out of Horace's enthusiasm for Sappho and Alcaeus? Was poetry 'with all its glory . . . the mainspring of the ode' (Fraenkel, 167)? Does the poem express Horace's new understanding of the essence of his art, as offering in its harmonies a release from grief and pain? Is it related to the spiritual nature of man, giving sense and order to life against a background of random senseless chance (Syndikus, 427)? Is Horace suggesting an unspoken thought that 'if he escapes the meaningless accidents of fortune . . . perhaps he himself may have the same capacity to enthral, console, and to survive' (Nisbet and Hubbard 1978: 205)?

These explanations are all attempts to find deep meanings in the poem, and they fail. First of all, Sappho is roughly handled. If Horace's intention is to praise Aeolic poetry and claim affinity with it, why is Sappho still complaining down there in the Underworld about the girls of Lesbos, who 'were Lesbians in more ways than one' as Nisbet and Hubbard argue, producing irrefutable evidence from the ancient texts? Horace has often let us know that lovers' complaints give him no pleasure. Besides, in line 33 it is the songs of Alcaeus, *illis carminibus*, which enthral the shades, and Horace himself clearly agreed with them (see *Odes* 1. 13. 3–9 and 1. 22. 23–4). The sound of Sappho's poignant reproaches fills the Latin of line 25 with an affecting alliteration of the letter -p-, as heard also in lines 3–4 and 37 of this ode. This makes an audible contrast with the forceful music of Alcaeus' poetry in lines 27–8. The metre, as determined by the quantity of the syllables, is as marked:

Ālcaēĕ, plēctrō dūră nāvīs,
  dūră fŭgaē mălă, dūră bēllī.

But the word accent adds a different rhythm to the verse:

Alcaée, pléctro dúra návis,
  dúra fúgae mála, dúra bélli.

This gives a succession of nine words whose stresses form nine trochees (compare 2. 19. 11–12, 3. 4. 65, and the fourteen accentual trochees at the beginning of *Odes* 4. 1). If the verse was read with any trace of the natural accent of the words, this surely sounded brisk (see Introduction, p. xxii and West 1995*c*: 106). If praise of Alcaeus as an inspiration for Horace's own poetic work is part of the purpose of this poem, there is another surprise. The music which the shades enjoy in line 32 is devoted to battles and exiled kings, and this fits well with Alcaeus' part in the uprising against Myrsilus, tyrant of Mytilene. But what sense does it make with lines 1 and 10–12 of the previous ode where Horace specifically declines to sing of wars, battles, and defeated kings? If Horace is claiming some affinity with Alcaeus why does he not mention Alcaeus' poems of love, as he has already done at 1. 32. 9–12? Some game is going on here.

There is one other even more powerful argument against solemn interpretations of this poem, and that is the frivolity of the description of the audience in the Underworld. It starts with a solemn, sacramental tone. There is a crowd of shades and they listen in holy silence. This alludes to the same procedure as Horace calls for at the beginning of the third book of *Odes*:

> odi profanum vulgus et arceo;
> favete linguis:
>
> I hate the profane crowd and keep it at a distance.
> Be favourable with your tongues.

But here in 2. 13 this is bluff, and soon exposed as such. First, at line 32 the crowd is somewhat contorted, dense with its shoulders and drinking with its ear in a compact, symmetrical line, *densum umeris bibit aure vulgus*. Second, when Cerberus is soothed by the music, the hundred-headed beast lets down its black ears. That makes 200 ears, and those who are sceptical of such calculations should remember that Cerberus normally has three heads. True, he has fifty in Hesiod, *Theogony* 312, and a hundred in Pindar, fragment 249b, *hekatongkephalas*, which Horace translates as *centiceps*, a 'grandiloquent and Grecizing compound' (Nisbet and Hubbard 1978). Horace chooses a different option at 2. 19. 31–2, where Cerberus has three heads, and again at 3. 11. 20 where he has a three-tongued mouth, *ore trilingui*. Third, it is strange that the same music as soothes Cerberus enlivens the snakes in the hair of the Furies, presumably an allusion to the coiling motions induced by snake-charming (contrast Virgil, *Aeneid* 7. 754, where Umbro puts snakes to sleep by singing to them). Fourth, in 37, another notably alliterative line, we read of Prometheus and Tantalus being deceived as to labour by the sweet sound. Again, given this playful context, this is slightly piquant. The suffering, *labor*, of Prometheus was to provide food from his liver for a vulture, and could, no doubt, have been *eased* by music. The labour of Tantalus, father of Pelops, was normally to reach for food and water which eternally receded, and could have *ceased*. But it was the taskmasters, not the sufferers, who were *deceived*; Prometheus and Tantalus must have been relieved, rather than deceived. The last allusion is to Orion, the great hunter, who in his life had pursued the fierce and the fearful, and still pursues them in death, but is distracted even from his pleasure by the songs of Alcaeus. Fifth, this case can be reinforced by a reading of a passage which Horace must have known in the work of his friend Virgil:

> at cantu commotae Erebi de sedibus imis
> umbrae ibant tenues simulacraque luce carentum,
> quam multa in foliis avium se milia condunt
> . . . .
> quin ipsae stupuere domus atque intima Leti
> Tartara caeruleosque implexae crinibus anguis
> Eumenides, tenuitque inhians tria Cerberus ora
> atque Ixionii vento rota constitit orbis.
>
> (Virgil, *Georgics* 4. 471–3, 481–4)

> But, roused by his song from the bottommost depths of Erebus,
> there were coming insubstantial shades and phantoms of those
> who do not have the light of life, like many thousands of birds
> flocking to hide in trees
> . . . .
> the very house of Death was struck dumb, the inmost chambers
> of Tartarus, and the Furies with blue snakes woven
> in their hair, Cerberus kept his three mouths gaping,
> and even the circle of Ixion's wheel was at rest in the wind.

Here, in this grave incantation, the shades come crowding to listen but we have no description of their shoulders or ear; there is stupefaction, but not of a dog; the serpents woven, *implexae*, in the hair of the Furies, in Horace are twisted, coiled, *torti*, in it, and in Horace they are stimulated; the watchdog listens without barking, with its three mouths open, a vivid but not burlesque detail. Horace's *jeux d'esprit* in the Underworld, particularly when read beside Virgil's account, clearly cannot be conveying any solemn message about poetry, about Horace's affiliation with the Aeolic poets, or about his understanding of his own poetic vocation or hopes of poetic immortality.

Poets do not need to preach and there is no need to believe that there must be a message. Sometimes they write as the poem takes them. The Muse has her own values, and tells her devotees when their poem works. Sometimes, even, they write for fun. Horace was Mercury's man (2. 17. 19) and Mercury was a mischief-maker (1. 10. 7–12). And sometimes, in the middle of cheerful poems they chill the blood, as Horace does here in lines 13–20.

In each generation which has cared for Latin and Greek poetry, scholars, some of them the greatest minds of their age, have busied themselves purging the manuscripts of errors and proposing emendations. They have tended towards excess. For instance, in the first stanza of this ode, Shackleton Bailey and Delz have followed Nisbet in putting *quicumque* between commas: 'the man who first planted you, whoever he was, . . . ', so spoiling the joke upon the originator, 'whoever first'. *Quicumque* cannot be read separate from *primum* (see *qui . . . primus*, *Odes* 1. 3. 10–12; *quicumque . . . primus*, Propertius, 1. 17. 13–14; and *qui . . . primus*, Seneca, *Medea* 301).

Again, strangely, this clear proposition about the Phoenician sailor in the Bosphorus has been vexed by conjectures. In line 15 the vivid word *ultra*, which means 'beyond', i.e. when he is beyond, past the straits, displeases for no good reason. In the same line a large number of corrections is offered for *Poenus*, Phoenician. The case against it is twofold. The first objection is that the adjective relates to Carthage, the colony of Tyre in Phoenicia, and not to Phoenicia itself. This is false. The word means 'Phoenician' at Propertius, 4. 3. 51 and plays with that meaning in the third line of the previous ode, 2. 12. The second is that it is strange to find the sailor with an adjective, *Poenus*, and not the soldier. But the rhetorical articulation of these three examples is perfectly rational and helpful to the understanding. Why does the first have an adjective and a noun, *navita . . . Poenus*, while the second has only a noun, *miles*, and the third only an adjective, *Parthus*? The answer is that the first example stands apart from the linked pair that follow, 'The *Phoenician sailor* is terrified of the Bosphorus; the *soldier* fears the retreating Parthian; the *Parthian* the Italian dungeon' (i.e. the *Robur Tullianum* in which prisoners of war were strangled after they had been dragged by the neck (2. 12. 12) through the streets of Rome in triumphal processions). Soldier and Parthian share the verb of fearing, *timet*, and this articulation is not strange or suspect. The soldier is an Italian and the Parthian is a soldier. We should reject any emendation of *Poenus*.

As so often, the modern emendation is inferior to the received text, but has helped us to understand it.

XIV

EHEU fugaces, Postume, Postume,
labuntur anni nec pietas moram
rugis et instanti senectae
adferet indomitaeque morti:

non si trecenis quotquot eunt dies,
amice, places illacrimabilem
Plutona tauris, qui ter amplum
Geryonen Tityonque tristi

compescit unda, scilicet omnibus,
quicumque terrae munere vescimur,
enaviganda, sive reges
sive inopes erimus coloni.

frustra cruento Marte carebimus
fractisque rauci fluctibus Hadriae,
frustra per autumnos nocentem
corporibus metuemus Austrum:

visendus ater flumine languido
Cocytos errans et Danai genus
infame damnatusque longi
Sisyphus Aeolides laboris:

linquenda tellus et domus et placens
uxor, neque harum quas colis arborum
te praeter invisas cupressos
ulla brevem dominum sequetur:

absumet heres Caecuba dignior
servata centum clavibus et mero
tinget pavimentum superbo,
pontificum potiore cenis.

This sombre poem tells us nothing we did not know. There is no escape from death. This is an 'Eat, drink, and be merry, for tomorrow you may die' without the eating, drinking, or merriment. But how can an utterance of a hundred-odd words of unrelieved misery, telling us nothing new, leave us with such a feeling of delight? It is clearly a great

XIV

Ah how quickly, Postumus, Postumus,
the years glide by, and piety will not delay
   the wrinkles and old age pressing at their heels,
      and death the unsubdued,

no, my friend, not if every day that passes, you sacrificed
three hundred bulls to appease Pluto, the god
   who cannot weep, who confines Tityos
      and the three-bodied giant Geryon

in the prison of those gloomy waters
that we know all of us must cross
   who feed upon the bounty of the earth,
      whether we be kings or poor tenant farmers.

In vain shall we avoid the bloody god of war
and the roaring breakers of the Adriatic.
   In vain autumn after long autumn shall we tremble
      for our health when the south wind blows.

We must go and see black Cocytus meandering
in its sluggish flow, the infamous daughters of Danaus,
   and Sisyphus, son of Aeolus,
      at his long sentence of hard labour.

We must leave the earth, our home,
and the wife we love, and none of these trees you tend
   except the hated cypresses
      will go with their short-lived master.

Your heir, worthier than yourself, will drink off
the Caecuban you laid down behind a hundred locks,
   and stain your paving with proud wine undiluted
      and too good for the banquets of priests.

poem. The difficulty is to say why, and scholars have risen to the challenge.

Williams (1968: 584–6) finds a dynamic in the movement from concrete detail to mythology and back to concrete detail in the last two stanzas. It begins with Postumus, moves to the universal at line 10, and glides back to Postumus at lines 21–2. These quiet changes of focus and of key suck us into the predicament of Postumus and remind us of our own. They are part of the drama of the poem.

Nisbet and Hubbard see it as 'a masterpiece of construction' with its great rolling first sentence on the inevitability of death, the futility of trying to escape it, and the need to cross a river in the Underworld. The next three stanzas cover the same ground with reference to all mankind, the futility of trying to escape death (13–16) and the inevitability of our journey to the Underworld and its river Cocytus. They note also that Horace 'balances his words with classical regularity'—land and water, for instance (9–11), kings and peasants (12), the repetition of 'in vain' (13, 15), the contrasts of going to see, leaving, and following (17, 21, 24), the laying down of wine and the swilling of it (25–6).

Such observations throw light on the structure and the drama of the poem, but the gloom remains: 'uncompromisingly stern' (Collinge, 49); 'no alleviation of a painful and haunting picture of the human condition' (Williams 1968: 115); 'Horace seems to be turning his back on life' (Nisbet and Hubbard 1978: 226); 'ruthlessly disconsolate' (Woodman 1967: 399). This doesn't sound like Horace. On close study, the poem turns out to have a lightness of tone and to be full of humour.

It starts with a lively metaphor. The years are in flight, *fugaces*, like the coward in battle at *Odes* 3. 2. 14. When we hear that wrinkles and old age are pressing hard, *instanti*, we are led to visualize a pursuit, and the next line of the Latin names the great enemy, death the undefeated, *indomitae*. After these three signposts to a battle scene *mora*, 'delay' falls aptly into place. It is used six times in Virgil, *Aeneid* 12, each time in a context of war, and in *Aeneid* 10. 428 the Etruscan warrior Abas is called the knot and delay of battle, *pugnae nodumque moramque*. Seneca at *Suasoriae* 2. 19 preserves a fragment of poetry: 'Hector, the delay of war, is fallen', *belli mora concidit Hector*. So then, wrinkles, old age, and death the *undefeated*, are formidable enemies, *pressing hard*. The years can put up no *obstacle*, they are *in flight*, and, as a final hint of war, their battle line *is breaking*, *labuntur* (as at Propertius, 4. 2. 53, 'I have seen battle lines breaking', *vidi ego labentis acies*). It would be wrong to see a military flavour in any one of these five possible military terms standing alone, particularly in *mora* or *labuntur*, but in this concentration each supports the other. Old age and death are gloomy topics, but Horace has found a sprightly way of talking about them.

Against this it is generally held that the repetition of the name of Postumus strikes a sad and serious note. No doubt such repetition *could* intensify the idea of sadness, but it certainly does not need to. Nisbet and Hubbard cite three examples of the repetition of a personal name, and these convey a range of different emotions: abiding love at Terence, *Andria* 282, admiring gratitude at *Adelphoe* 256, and mocking astonishment at Plautus, *Miles Gloriosus* 415. The repetition conveys intensity of emotion but does not reveal what emotion is being felt. For that we have to read on. The second stanza settles the question. A hecatomb is the sacrifice of a hundred animals, conducted mainly on great state occasions. A sacrifice of 300 oxen was performed after a series of calamitous defeats by Hannibal which culminated in the defeat at Lake Trasimene in 217 BC. For an individual to perform a hecatomb would be extraordinary. To sacrifice 300 animals every day that passes would be absurd, and the absurdity is heightened by the order of the words in Latin. After *trecenis* near the beginning of the clause we wait in some suspense till it ends with *tauris* and we know that it is a matter of 300 bulls. Surely it stands to reason that in any language repetition can be used to express the intensity of any feeling. Here *Postume, Postume* is spoken not in inconsolable sadness, but with a rueful smile, and a shake of the head—'You know it, Postumus, Postumus, and I know it too.' Here is a wry acceptance of the truth, and, as so often in Horace's words addressed to friends, a note of gentle teasing. This impression is confirmed in what follows—the impossibility of placating a god who cannot weep, and the triply huge Geryon whose claim to fame was that he had three trunks to his body, whereas the single body of Tityos who follows without an epithet was known to have covered 9 acres in the Underworld (Homer, *Odyssey* 11. 577 and *Lucretius*, 3. 988). They have both had to go to the Underworld. What chance has Postumus of escaping it?

In lines 13–14 there is no mistaking the sounds of battle and 'the broken waves of the raucous Adriatic',

> frustra cruento marte carebimus
> fractisque rauci fluctibus Hadriae.

These rough sounds (8r + 6c + 5t) at 15–16 are followed by the creeping dangers of the heat of an Italian autumn in a different key (5m + 3n). Scepticism is in order but this interpretation can be defended. Lucretius, in a passage which Horace had already drawn upon in *Satires* 1. 1. 117–19, used similar (and untranslatable) effects to mimic those who mourn excessively for the death of their loved ones:

> 'misero misere' aiunt 'omnia ademit una dies'
> . . . .

> 'insatiabiliter deflevimus aeternumque
> nulla dies nobis maerorem e pectore demet.'
>
> (Lucretius, 3. 898 and 907–8)
>
> 'One day,' they say, 'has wretchedly taken everything away
> from the poor wretch'
> . . . .
> 'we have mourned insatiably for you, and no day
> will ever take the undying grief from our hearts.'

Nearer home is Horace's own gentler mockery at *Epistles* 1. 7. 5–13, which came out in 20 BC, three years after these odes. Here he is making excuses to Maecenas for not being in Rome in August,

> dum ficus prima calorque
> dissignatorem decorat lictoribus atris,
> dum pueris omnis pater et matercula pallet,
> officiosaque sedulitas et opella forensis
> adducit febris et testamenta resignat.
> quodsi bruma nives Albanis illinet agris,
> ad mare descendet vates tuus et sibi parcet
> contractusque leget: te, dulcis amice, reviset
> cum Zephyris, si concedes, et harundine prima.
>
> while the first fig and the heat
> are adorning the undertaker with black-clad attendants,
> while every father and doting mother is pale with worry over their sons,
> and conscientious diligence and footling little forum duties
> bring on the fevers and open wills.
> But if midwinter smears snow on Alban fields,
> your prophet-priest will down to the sea and look after himself,
> curling up and reading. He'll come back to see you, if you allow it,
> dear friend, with the Zephyrs and the first swallow.

Here, too, as in *Odes* 2. 14 we have mockery on the subject of the dangers of autumn in Italy, and Horace uses a similar battery of sound effects. There is humour in suggesting that a fig could decorate an undertaker, and the black cloaks of his attendants make an odd decoration. Alliteration, audible in lines 5–6, continues when we look away from the sombre black of the attendants to the parents pale because of their sons, *pueris . . . pater . . . pallet*. The affecting diminutive *matercula* is guyed immediately by *opella*, referring to the fiddling little bits of forum business which remain to be conducted in August. Neither of these two diminutives occurs elsewhere in Horace. Part of the fun lies in the contrast with the mighty polysyllables of line 8 (compare Lucretius, 3. 907 above), conveying the tedious trivia which bring on the fevers and open the wills. The Romans, being more sensitive to personification than we are, would visualize Conscientiousness and Drudgery busily doing so. In his commentary on the opening of the wills in line 9, Mayer observes that 'this is a humorous way of saying that the fevered die' but not another word to suggest the humour that runs all through this passage and is vital to the interpretation of the poem. Mayer reports that 'The unusual rhythm of line 8 with only a fourth-foot caesura may be expressive of anxiety (Nilsson, 84) or restlessness (Kiessling).' He has read the commentators but has not listened to the Latin. The tedious trivialities of line 8 rattle along in a line with five dactyls, and their mortal consequences fill a line opening with four spondees:

— ⏑⏑ — ⏑⏑ — ⏑⏑ — ⏑⏑ — ⏑⏑ — ~
— — — — — — — — — ⏑⏑ — ~.

An over-solemn approach destroys the poetry of Horace's *Epistles*. When Horace says that he will come back with the Zephyrs and the first swallow, it is not enough to tell us that the west wind and the swallow are first found together in Leonidas of Tarentum. We should be catching Horace's smile as he sees himself curled up to hibernate and then returning with the migrating birds in spring. Solemnity leads to misunderstandings. Horsfall is more alert to the humour of this passage than other commentators and as a result propounds a much more sensitive and plausible interpretation of the relationship between Maecenas and Horace, stressing the playful delicacy of Horace's tone, his independence, and Maecenas' acceptance of it.

Similar features in *Odes* 2. 14. 13–16 confirm the tone of mockery of the maudlin which we have already perceived in the second stanza. This poem is not entirely dismal.

There is a typical clash between the hoarseness of the Adriatic in line 14 and the languid flow of the black river Cocytus in the Underworld in lines 15–16, a clash more acute if, like John Milton, we know the etymology of the word. The Adriatic is hoarse, but the Cocytus is the river of wailing, from the Greek *kokuo*, 'a river named of lamentation loud' (*Paradise Lost*, v. 279). Cicero had already had fun with this etymology by mocking the roaring of the Cocytus, *Cocyti fremitus*, at *Tusculan Disputations* 1. 10.

In the next two stanzas lines 17–20 form a triad which must be visited, *visendus*, and lines 21–4 a triad which must be left behind, *linquenda*.

Now Horace moves from the universal to the personal. Postumus must leave his dear wife and go amongst villains like the daughters of Danaus, of whom forty-nine out of fifty murdered their bridegrooms on the wedding night, and Sisyphus, 'the craftiest of men' (Homer, *Iliad* 6. 153). But even this gloomy prospect is touched with humour. The long (an understatement) sentence of hard labour served for all eternity by Sisyphus in rolling his boulder up the hill and always failing to reach the top is a piquant contrast to the life of leisure enjoyed by a Roman aristocrat in his villa, and suggested by the tree-tending that follows. And why at the mention of *Sisyphus Aeolides*, contrary to normal practice, is the proper name accompanied by the patronymic? No doubt this adds a note of epic solemnity, but we may also remember the legend that Ulysses was the bastard son of Sisyphus, himself son of Aeolus. So Virgil, *Aeneid* 6. 529 refers to Ulysses as *hortator scelerum Aeolides*, 'that ringleader of atrocity, Ulysses, of the windking's line' in Fitzgerald's amazing translation. This is bad company, a far cry from civilized and amiable people like Postumus and his family.

In lines 21–4 Postumus must leave the wife he loves, and the trees he tends, and the only thing that will follow him to his grave will be the loathed cypresses, *invisas cypressos*, which will decorate his house when he dies, be carried in his funeral procession, and grow above his grave.

Such polar tensions, as we have often seen in this book, are part of the poetic logic of the piece and it would be a pity to ignore two elusive examples. The contrast between the Adriatic and 'black Cocytus, meandering with its languid flow' invites us to visualize the dazzling blue of the Italian seas, and when the wine stains the paving at the end of the poem, the wine must surely be red and the paving white marble. (This is to posit an extension of the *schema Horatianum*, as discussed on 2. 3. 9.)

In many of the poems of this book the interpretation depends upon the character of the addressee. By a feat of learning and ingenuity Nisbet and Hubbard propose a convincing identification for this Postumus. Unfortunately nothing relevant to the ode is known about his character or career. In an attempt to fill the gap it has been suggested that he was morose, superstitious, and, worst of all, a hoarder of wine. This is all pressing the poem too hard. The early part of the poem does not imply that he hoped to postpone his death by extreme religious observance and hypochondria. The tone is too light and witty for that. Similarly, to lay down Caecuban and keep it secure is not neurosis or stinginess, but prudence. According to Athenaeus, 1. 26c–27d Falernian needed from fifteen to twenty years to mature and Horace asks for a Caecuban twenty-six years old at *Odes* 3. 28. 8. During that time the master of a large household of slaves would have been very foolish if he did not keep his cellar secure. It would be as unhumorous to suppose that Postumus had a hundred locks to his cellar as to believe that he was tempted to kill 300 oxen every day. Horace is smiling.

All we can safely deduce about Postumus from the poem is that he was a married man with a town house and a villa, and that he liked his trees and his wine. Nor can we be sure that a young rapscallion was waiting to inherit and drink the cellar dry. By the *Lex Voconia* of 169 BC a wealthy Roman was forbidden to leave his property to a woman, and by the *Lex Falcidia* of 40 BC he had to name an heir who would receive at least a quarter of the estate. It is the result of these legal provisions that Horace is here predicting, again with some exaggeration. A problem arises with Horace's assertion that this heir will be worthier. Again, this has been taken as a negative reflection on Postumus—praise of the heir before the death of the testator. Implausible. Look how this heir treats wine. It seems rather to be a dry comment by Horace on the amorality of life. The worthy die and the unworthy inherit and despoil their inheritance. This happens, and Horace is facing the truth. It may happen to Postumus, and to sharpen the moral Horace says that it will, but that is no support for those who find criticism of Postumus or take the view that in the last two stanzas Horace is turning his back on life.

We all know his basic argument. Life is brief and nothing can prolong it. Therefore enjoy it. This conclusion is so frequent in his poetry, so memorable and unanswerable, that readers are bound to hear it coming. This is no dirge. It is a buoyant, realistic, lively poem, and its energy sets problems for the imagination of the reader throughout. The last of these is to supply the missing conclusion. The positive message is there, clear but unstated, in the last two stanzas. Horace is not notable as a merchant of gloom, but he is a master of unstatement.

XV

Iam pauca aratro iugera regiae
moles relinquent, undique latius
  extenta visentur Lucrino
    stagna lacu, platanusque caelebs

evincet ulmos; tum violaria et
myrtus et omnis copia narium
  spargent olivetis odorem
    fertilibus domino priori;

tum spissa ramis laurea fervidos
excludet ictus. non ita Romuli
  praescriptum et intonsi Catonis
    auspiciis veterumque norma.

privatus illis census erat brevis,
commune magnum: nulla decempedis
  metata privatis opacam
    porticus excipiebat Arcton,

nec fortuitum spernere caespitem
leges sinebant, oppida publico
  sumptu iubentes et deorum
    templa novo decorare saxo.

Contrasts, as we have often seen, can be a crucial element in Horace's *Odes*. Here, for instance, the first part of this poem contrasts the traditional Italian landscape of farms, vineyards, and olive groves with a future Italy covered with ornamental gardens, while the second part contrasts the ideal of the hardy poverty of life in the early republic with the luxuries of the modern villa.

By setting the first part in the future Horace frees himself to exaggerate and give an edge to his satire. A shortage of ploughland was never a real possibility but it makes a striking opening to the poem. The Lucrine Lake on the Bay of Naples was the site of the greatest engineering feat of the age. To provide a secure harbour for Octavian's fleet in the war against Sextus Pompeius in 37–36 BC, Agrippa reinforced the natural barrier between the lake and the sea and cut a navigable channel from the Lucrine through to the deep-water berth of Lake Avernus. In celebrating this extraordinary achievement at *Georgics* 2. 161–4, Virgil describes

XV

Huge palaces will soon leave few acres
for the plough. On every side fishpools
  broader than the Lucrine Lake
    will meet the eye and the bachelor plane

will push out the elms. Then myrtles and beds of violet
and everything the nose could desire
  will scatter perfumes where the old farmer
    had his fertile olive groves.

Dense laurel will then shut out the fiery shafts
of the sun. This is not what was prescribed by the auspices
  taken by Romulus and unshaven Cato
    and by the rule of the ancients.

Their private wealth was small.
Their public wealth was great. No portico laid out
  by ten-foot rod caught the dense northern shade
    for private citizens,

and laws commanded them not to despise the turf
beneath their feet, but to beautify at common cost
  their towns and the temples of their gods
    with freshly quarried stone.

the salt sea rushing into Lake Avernus (Paget, 163–5). In Horace, by contrast, the new artificial lakes, elaborate as they were and sometimes of salt water, are called *stagna*, a word which hints that they were landlocked and nasty. The next contrast is between the plane and the elm. Elms were often grown as props for vines, but the leaves of the plane tree, *platanus*, are so broad (*platys* is the Greek for broad) that the tree is useless for vines, and good only to keep the sun off the rich. The union of elm or poplar with the vine is often thought of as a marriage, as in *Epodes* 2. 9–10, where the countryman marries the tall poplars with the grown off-spring of the vines,

ergo aut adulta vitium propagine
altas maritat populos.

Quintilian plays with the same metaphor at 8. 3. 8, *sterilem platanum tonsasque myrtos quam maritam ulmum et uberes oleas praeoptaverim?* 'Would

I prefer the sterile plane and shaven myrtles to a wedded elm and fruitful olives?' Quintilian's satire makes explicit the human implication; Horace touches it lightly with the word *caelebs*, bachelor.

The ridicule continues in the second stanza with the grotesque description of the fragrant garden where, literally, 'every abundance of noses scatters a smell' in what were once olive groves. Is this abundance a harvest owned by noses? Are these fragrant flowers scattering smell where once the farmer scattered grain seed between his olive trees? Or are they seen as effete slaves swinging perfumed censers at a banquet? One thing is certain—that Horace looks upon this abundance as sterility. We have already seen that the wealthy need plane trees to keep the sun off them, and now in line 9 they need the laurel and so sensitive are they that they feel the rays of the sun as burning blows, *fervidos ictus*, presumably from blazing arrows. How different the busy Sabine or Apulian farmer's wife, scorched by the sun at *Epodes* 2. 41–2,

Sabina qualis aut perusta solibus
  pernicis uxor Apuli.

The poem is not an undifferentiated denunciation of modern luxury. In the middle of line 10, Horace begins to leave villa gardens and turns towards villa architecture. He also leaves the future and turns to the past. 'This is not', he says, 'what was prescribed by the auspices of Romulus.' This takes us back to the story of the foundation of Rome, to the auspices conducted by Romulus and his twin brother Remus to determine which of them would rule the new city and give it his name. Remus saw six vultures. Romulus immediately saw twelve. More relevant to this poem, perhaps, is the information provided by Cicero at *De Republica* 2. 26 that Romulus allocated land to the citizens, and by Varro, *De Re Rustica* 1. 10. 2 that he decreed that 2 iugera of land was to be the amount that could be transmitted by inheritance. But so intense in Livy's account of the life of Romulus (1. 6–16) is the stress upon his scrupulous observance of religious ritual, that contemporary readers would have found no difficulty in taking this to suggest that he observed the auspices in order to determine land boundaries and win the blessing of the gods for them.

The first Roman to have a daily shave was Scipio Africanus the Younger (185/4–129 BC) and he was fifty years younger than Cato the Censor. Cato's beard in line 11 would have been a symbol of his resistance to all things Greek and all things luxurious. And he made it quite clear that he was not afraid of the sun. In a surviving fragment (128) of a speech he explains how from the very beginning he was abstinent for the whole of his youth, living in parsimony, in drudgery, and in hardship, tilling the soil, breaking Sabine rocks with flints (if that is what the Latin means), and sowing them with seed, *ego iam a principio in parsimonia atque in duritia atque industria omnem adulescentiam abstinui agro colendo, saxis Sabinis silicibus repastinandis atque conserendis*. Like the muster of republican heroes in *Odes* 1. 12. 33–46, Cato stands as a model of hard work, harsh poverty, and moral severity. He, too, was famous for his observance of ritual duties. He, too, would have taken the auspices.

The transition to architecture is skilfully managed, and the pivot comes in line 12 at *veterum norma*, the rule of the ancients, *norma* being strictly a set-square. There is no difficulty about associating Cato with rules or measuring instruments. His *De Agri Cultura* is largely a list of commands, and chapters 10–13 list the equipment required for an oliveyard of 250 *iugera* and a vineyard of 100 *iugera*, and in each inventory there are more than a hundred headings. The ancient farm-builder would have used a set-square, but the modern villa architect, working to a much larger module, requires the new-fangled *decempeda*, a 10-foot rod with metal ferrules. Nor are we finished with sneers at those who are afraid of the sun. In the old days no portico used to trap the dense or thick Arctos, *opacam Arcton*. Arctos is the north, from the name *Arctos*, the Bear, given to the constellation we call the Plough. The verb *excipere* is a hunting term. The Romans netted an area, and then waited with their spears at the gap in the net to ambush, *excipere*, the terrified game as they were driven out. At *Odes* 3. 12. 12, for example, the young man is swift to ambush a wild boar, *excipere aprum*. Here the wealthy villa-owner provides a portico where he and his friends and family can ambush the bear, that is, catch the northern shade. When Horace calls it dense, he just stops short of forcing us to think of it as shaggy. Such jokes based on the literal interpretation of astronomical terms are common in Latin poetry, for example at *Odes* 1. 26. 3 and 3. 29. 18–19.

The poem ends with an evocation of a primitive Italy of turf houses and, in contrast, walled towns, with temples of stone quarried for the purpose, a vision which Virgil sees in the Italy of his own day, and which, once seen, is never forgotten:

> adde tot egregias urbes operumque laborem,
> tot congesta manu praeruptis oppida saxis
> fluminaque antiquos subterlabentia muros.
>
> (*Georgics* 2. 155–7)

> Think too of all those noble cities and works of men,
> all these towns piled up by their hands on precipices of rock
> and rivers gliding beneath their ancient walls.

An important element in the ode is its ethical content, notably the theme of moral degeneracy. This is well dealt with by the commentators who trace the influence of previous philosophers. Here it seems more useful to follow up a remark by Nisbet and Hubbard (1978: 243), 'By implication Horace favours Augustan ideology by denouncing the magnificence of independent noblemen.' With what ears would Augustus have heard this poem?

From the beginning he would have approved of the sentiments expressed about the decline of Italian agriculture. The idealization of old Italy would also have suited his diplomatic policy, since he presented himself as the leader of Italy, and Italy was an important part of his power-base. (See, for example, his own official account of his achievements in his *Res Gestae* 25 and the notes by Brunt and Moore.) Still in this first stanza, Augustus would warmly have sympathized with the view that it would be a disgrace if villa-owners had artificial pools which were larger than the Lucrine Lake, where he had built the vast harbour which had enabled him to win a desperately close war against what he held to be the forces of evil. This was a war in which he came near to death, and it was his hard-won victory which made possible the Roman renaissance that was part of his policy when Horace was writing these poems. He would not have approved of fishponds which dwarfed his greatest engineering achievement. A third outrage, in the eyes of Augustus, was the bachelor planes. Trees in Latin are feminine in gender and when fruitful elms are ousted by bachelor planes, grammatical gender takes on a sexual undertone, as in *Odes* 1. 24. 6–7. Augustus disapproved of wealthy men who devoted themselves to selfish pleasure instead of marrying and having children, a disapproval which he would later embody in the Julian Laws of 18 BC, adumbrated by Horace in *Odes* 3. 3–6, celebrated in his *Secular Hymn* (17 BC) and repeatedly cited in *Odes* 4 (13 BC). These trees have this touch of symbolism to them, and perhaps the prejudice against the pleasure-loving bachelors is continued in the sneering references to perfumes in the stanza which follows.

The third stanza is even more clearly Augustan. The mother of Romulus was Ilia, the priestess queen of Virgil, *Aeneid* 1. 273, because of her name presumably a descendant of Ilus/Iulus and a daughter of the Julian kings of Alba Longa. Romulus therefore is a member of the same family as Augustus. When Octavian took the name Augustus in January 27 BC, he had been tempted instead to choose to call himself Romulus (Suetonius, *Augustus* 7). Like Romulus, he respected and observed the rituals of religion at every point in his career, making it be known, for example, that Roman commanders who won victories during his rule were fighting under his auspices (*Res Gestae* 4). Rome began when Romulus took the auspices and observed twelve vultures. Rome began again when Augustus entered upon his first consulship, took the auspices, and observed twelve vultures (Suetonius, *Augustus* 95). He would also have warmed at the mention of Cato the Censor since, like Cato, he punctiliously performed the duties of censor (*Res Gestae* 6), striving to purge the Senate and the Equestrian Order of those deemed unworthy. In general, Augustus believed in the value of examples, as is clear from Suetonius, *Augustus* 31 (see also *Res Gestae* 8. 5 and Zanker, 210):

> Next to the immortal gods he paid honour to the memory of those leaders who had made Roman rule great from the smallest beginnings. And so he revived the memory of all their achievements by means of inscriptions intended to last, and dedicated statues of all of them in triumphal garb in the porticos on each side of his Forum proclaiming also in an edict that he had so designed this so that they should be the standards which the citizens of Rome should demand of himself, while he lived, and of the leaders of ages still to come.

Cato won a triumph for his work in Spain in 194 BC, and was probably one of the great Romans whose statue stood in triumphal garb in the Forum of Augustus.

In view of Augustus' claim in *Res Gestae* 20 that in 28 BC he restored eighty-two temples within the city of Rome, we cannot but read the last stanza of this ode as an unmistakable tribute from the poet to the Princeps. Augustus himself boasted, with some exaggeration, that he found Rome brick and left it marble (Suetonius, *Augustus* 28). Horace's contrast between the turf-built house in the country and the temples in the towns of Italy built of fresh-cut stone is a compliment deliberately aimed off the target, but there can have been no doubt that contemporary Romans would have taken the point. The poem is panegyric, and all the more effective for offering no explicit tribute. It has no addressee but everyone would have known that it was about Augustus.

XVI

Otium divos rogat in patenti
prensus Aegaeo, simul atra nubes
condidit lunam neque certa fulgent
sidera nautis;

otium bello furiosa Thrace,
otium Medi pharetra decori,
Grosphe, non gemmis neque purpura ve-
nale nec auro.

non enim gazae neque consularis
summovet lictor miseros tumultus
mentis et curas laqueata circum
tecta volantis.

vivitur parvo bene, cui paternum
splendet in mensa tenui salinum
nec levis somnos timor aut cupido
sordidus aufert.

quid brevi fortes iaculamur aevo
multa? quid terras alio calentis
sole mutamus? patriae quis exsul
se quoque fugit?

scandit aeratas vitiosa navis
Cura nec turmas equitum relinquit,
ocior cervis et agente nimbos
ocior Euro.

laetus in praesens animus quod ultra est
oderit curare et amara lento
temperet risu; nihil est ab omni
parte beatum.

abstulit clarum cita mors Achillem,
longa Tithonum minuit senectus,
et mihi forsan, tibi quod negarit,
porriget hora.

XVI

The man caught in the open Aegean asks the gods
for peace of mind, as soon as a dark cloud obscures
the moon and stars no longer shine
    to give sure guidance to sailors.

'Peace,' asks Thrace so furious in war.
'Peace,' cry the Medes with their gorgeous quivers.
But peace cannot be bought with jewels, Grosphus,
    nor with purple or gold.

No eastern treasure and no consul's lictor
disperse the riots of a troubled mind
or the cares fluttering
    round coffered ceilings.

A man lives well on little if his father's salt-cellar
shines on his modest table,
and if fear and sordid desires do not disturb
    his easy sleep.

Why do we brave fellows throw so many javelins
in our short lives? Why travel to places
warmed by a different sun? What exile from his native land
    has ever escaped himself?

Corroding care boards the bronze-plated ship
and keeps pace with squadrons of horsemen,
swifter than deer, swifter than the east wind
    driving the clouds.

The mind which finds delight in the present moment
should not worry about what is to come,
but should dilute all bitterness with a slow smile.
    Nothing is perfect in every part.

An early death carried off the glorious Achilles,
a long old age reduced Tithonus,
and time will perhaps hold out to me
    what it denies to you.

te greges centum Siculaeque circum
mugiunt vaccae, tibi tollit hinnitum
apta quadrigis equa, te bis Afro
murice tinctae

vestiunt lanae: mihi parva rura et
spiritum Graiae tenuem Camenae
Parca non mendax dedit et malignum
spernere vulgus.

Epicurus (341–270 BC) taught that if we have true understanding we guide every choice by calculating the health of our bodies and the avoidance of disturbance of our minds. The good life does not include fear of our fellow men, of gods, or death, or of an afterlife, nor is it consistent with desire for wealth, luxurious living, fame, or power. Such fears and desires are storms of the soul.

These Epicurean ideas fill this poem from its very first word, *otium*, ease, conveying in Latin that freedom from disturbance, *ataraxia*, *hesuchia*, *schole*, which is the central objective of the Epicurean life. But it seems that Horace had in his mind not the Greek writings of Epicurus, but the *De Rerum Natura* of his pupil Lucretius (99–55 BC). For example, the first climax of the ode at line 13 comes in the very words of Lucretius at 5. 1117–19, 'for if a man directs his life by true reason, his supreme wealth is to live contentedly with little', *vivere parce aequo animo*. But Horace's main inspiration was the opening of the second book:

> suave mari magno turbantibus aequora ventis
> e terra magnum alterius spectare laborem.
>
> (Lucretius, 2. 1–2)

> Sweet it is when the winds are disturbing the levels of the great ocean
> to see from land the mighty struggles of somebody else.

These disturbances and struggles are soon defined, and I italicize Latin words which closely resemble the passages in Horace's ode:

> certare ingenio, contendere nobilitate
> noctes atque dies niti praestante *labore*
> *ad summas emergere opes rerumque potiri.*
> . . . .
> nonne videre
> nil aliud sibi naturam latrare nisi utqui
> *corpore* seiunctus *dolor absit*, *mens*que fruatur

Odes 2.16

Round you are lowing a hundred flocks
and Sicilian cattle. For you is neighing the mare
fit to draw a four-horse chariot. You are clad
in wool twice dyed

by African shellfish. To me Fate, untreacherous,
has given a small farm and the modest breath
of a Greek Camena, and has allowed me to despise
the malice of the mob.

iucundo sensu *cura* semota *metu*que?
ergo *corpoream ad naturam pauca videmus*
esse opus omnino, quae demant cumque dolorem

. . . .

nec domus *argento* fulget *auroque* renidet
nec citharae reboant *laqueata* aurataque *tecta*

. . . .

quapropter quoniam nil nostro in corpore *gazae*
proficiunt neque nobilitas nec *gloria regni*
quod superest, *animo* quoque nil prodesse putandum
si non forte tuas legiones per loca campi
fervere cum videas . . .

(Lucretius, 2. 11–13, 16–21, 27–8, 37–41)

pitting talent against talent, vying in breeding,
struggling night and day with the utmost drudgery
to rise to the heights of wealth and to gain power.

. . . .

to think that men fail to see
that all Nature demands is that pain should be far removed
from the body, and that the mind should enjoy
a sense of pleasure, remote from care and fear.
We see therefore that for our bodily nature only very few things
are needed, only those which can remove pain,

. . . .

nor does the house sparkle with silver and glow with gold
nor do gilded and coffered ceilings boom back the noise of the lyre.

. . . .

And so, since treasures of the east do no good
to our bodies, nor breeding nor the glory of kingly power,
we must then believe that they do nothing for our minds either,
if, when you look at your legions seething on the plain . . .

The resemblances do not end there. Fear and care, *metus* and *cura*, recur in 45–6 and again in 48, where they are not daunted by the clashing of arms and mix with kings and potentates, showing no reverence for the gleam of gold or the splendour of purple.

Horace follows Lucretius closely, but the differences are more important than the resemblances. Consider only three, the logic, the imagery, and the tone. The logical structure of Lucretius is clearly signposted. You know where you are when he is arguing, because he says what he is going to prove, proves it, and then says what he has proved with repetitions throughout to bear the logic (see West 1976). Horace, on the other hand, is not an evangelist but a ruminator. There are many different ways of analysing the argument of this ode. Nisbet and Hubbard follow an analysis which finds five groups of two stanzas each. Kiessling has three sections breaking after line 12 and after line 28. I read the poem as though the first break comes after line 16, when Horace has argued that wealth and power do not bring ease but the simple life does. The second section repeats this contrast in different terms from line 17 to line 24, where the poem moves towards a new proposition—that nothing is wholly perfect, supported by two mythological illustrations and ending with the examples of Grosphus and Horace. These disputed divisions are no discredit to Horace or to the scholars who perceive them. On the contrary, one of Horace's arts is to blur his translations and wrongfoot the reader, so achieving an informal tone and avoiding the pedagogic manner.

The second difference to be noted here is that the imagery of Lucretius is always a weapon of argument (West 1994*b*, particularly pages 136–9). His metaphors, similes, analogies, and examples are there to give visible force, clarity, and credibility to the propositions he is advancing. He is an evangelist and a teacher and his imagery drives home his lesson. In Horace the pictures keep changing, merging, fading, recurring, helping him to look all round his ideas, to inspect them with pleasure, humour, wit, and all manner of emotional hints. Finally, the tone is clearly different. Lucretius is unsurpassed in Latin for sublimity and passion, and he is a zealot. Not so Horace.

These differences begin to emerge with a consideration of the first word in the poem, *otium*. In this heavily Epicurean context, it is clearly a translation of Epicurus' *ataraxia*, freedom from disturbance, but in its three occurrences in these first two stanzas it is not used in a strict philosophical sense. In the first place it comes heavy with literary allusion. The greatest beginner of poems is Pindar, and his eighth Pythian begins with a rapt address to *Hesuchia*, 'Peace', which is a word later used by Epicurus as a synonym for his *ataraxia*:

> Loving-hearted Peace,
> daughter of Justice and giver of greatness to cities,
> holder of the mighty keys of counsel and of war . . .

But Horace has not only borrowed a whiff of sublimity from Pindar. Yet again, as in *Odes* 1. 13, 16, and 22, he has shown, by contrast, how puny is the self-indulgence of his contemporary Catullus:

> Otium, Catulle, tibi molestum est:
> otio exultas nimiumque gestis:
> otium et reges prius et beatas
> perdidit urbes.
>
> (Catullus, 51. 13–16)

> Idleness is bad for you, Catullus.
> Because of idleness you are too lively and lusty:
> Idleness has already destroyed kings
> and prosperous cities.

Quite apart from such reminiscences, which some readers would have caught and others not, in Horace's ode the word *otium* presents different facets in the three different contexts. When the sailor on the Aegean is so quick to ask for it at the first sign of a storm, we must be reminded of the frightened merchant just south of the Aegean in *Odes* 1. 15–18, who praises *otium* and the countryside round his native town in Italy, but can't bear poverty, and so is soon rebuilding his shattered fleet. The first word in *Odes* 2. 16, therefore, charged as it is with Epicurus, Pindar, and Catullus, reminds us also of a spurious and temporary longing for the peaceful, simple life of leisure in the Italian countryside. In line 5 the Epicurean allusion persists and the frenzy of the Thracians hints at their non-Epicurean activities, their violence, drunkenness and practice of ecstatic religion, but uppermost is the sense of peace as opposed to war, the fourth definition in the *Oxford Latin Dictionary*. In line 6 the ornamental quivers of the Persians continue this theme, but also begin a glide towards the rejection of wealth and the praise of the simple life, in the address to Grosphus in the next two lines. This simple Epicurean life is best lived at home, and the Aegean, the Thracians, and the Persians in these opening stanzas are preparing us for that dislike of travel which will be explicit at lines 13 and 18–20. This mode of presentation is impressionism, rather than argument. Similarly the golden Persian quivers encrusted with jewels, and their warriors clad in purple, suggest that the storm-tossed sailor in the first stanza is risking his life for profit derived from trading in luxury goods including purple dyes. In lines 7–9 this purple has become the senatorial stripe on the hem of the consul's toga, and there will be another glimpse of purple in lines 36–7 of the poem. This is philosophy by insinuation and by shimmering pictures, totally different from the dialectical artillery of Lucretius. And it is pointed at a person. The name of Grosphus comes at a crucial moment in the poem.

In line 9 *gazae*, translated as 'eastern treasures', is a Persian loanword, and therefore a feint at the sailor merchant, another argument by insinuation. This is followed by a glimpse of the consul's officer (and the lictors also wore purple) clearing a path with his rod for the great man as he walks through the streets between his home and the Forum where he conducts the affairs of state. The throng of wretched Romans, no doubt making appeals and offering petitions, merges into the unhappy confusions of his mind, and when he sits at splendid dinners there are winged creatures fluttering under the coffered ceilings. We may think of bats, for their sinister, lurching movements.

After this complex and crushing indictment of wealth and power, Horace speaks as plainly as could be the praises of the simple life, 'it is lived well with little', *vivitur parvo bene*. Yet Epicurus does not recommend a squalid, grinding poverty but rather the gracious, loving harmony of life in the Epicurean Garden, as suggested in Lucretius' description of the Epicurean picnic by a flowing stream at 2. 29–33, quoted in the comments on *Odes* 2. 3. Horace has translated the conditions of this commune into Latin and put forward his own ideal of *ataraxia*—a farm which has been in the family for generations. They have not been rich, but they are of some substance. Their salt-cellar is an heirloom, and since it shines, it is not of earthenware, but of some well-polished metal which is precious to them.

Once again, in lines 17–26, the strenuous non-Epicurean life is attacked, and the section ends with a plain statement of the Epicurean ideal. The general message is the same and the arch of sense is identical, but it is no mechanical repeat. The main target now is travel and the tempo changes. Lines 17–20 consist of three rhetorical questions, and, as is common in a succession of questions or exclamations, urgency is added by enjambement, as they stride over the line endings. The first of the questions resuscitates the notion of the folly of war, and has a little smile for Grosphus, since *grosphos* is the Greek for a throwing spear, but whereas Lucretius mocks and denounces, Horace includes himself in the charge, 'Why do *we* brave fellows throw so many javelins in our short lives?' Now those who exchange their own homes for lands warmed by a different sun are gently teased. There is, of course, only one sun. Such people are baying for the moon. 'Those who run across the sea change their sky, not their minds', *caelum non animum mutant qui trans mare currunt*, as Horace writes at *Epistles* 1. 11. 27. In line 20 when Horace asks if any exile ever escapes himself, we hear again the voice of Lucretius. In his satire on the restlessness of men at 3. 1053–75, he scoffs at the man who rushes from city to villa and villa to city for running away from himself—the person, of course, whom he cannot run away from, *quem scilicet, ut fit, effugere haud potis est*.

The bronze-plated ships and the squadrons of cavalry, of *equites*, pose a problem. They are normally taken to refer to war, and in favour of that interpretation, it could be argued that here too Horace is influenced by Lucretius, who argues at 2. 40–5 that it does not confer happiness upon a commander to see his troops or fleets arrayed before him. On the other hand there is another picture which may also be in the frame. On 15 July every year the Equites, the Roman Knights, sometimes to the number of 5,000, paraded arrayed by tribes and centuries, before the censors, a procedure renewed and assiduously practised by Augustus (Suetonius, *Life* 38. 3). This must have been an unforgettable spectacle, 'a noble sight, worthy of the greatness of the Roman Empire' (Dionysius of Halicarnassus, 6. 13. 4). These wealthy equestrians also owned seaside villas, and the paintings of the seaboard at the Bay of Naples show imposing pleasure craft moored at, or plying between, their private wharves. In favour of such an allusion to the *travectio* of the equestrian order is the power of the image. These extremely wealthy Romans may have cruised on their glittering pleasure ships, but corroding care boarded with them, *scandit aeratas vitiosa navis Cura*; they may have paraded through the streets of Rome crowned with olive leaves and attired in purple robes with scarlet stripes, but always there was a dark presence at their backs. The picture comes from a very similar passage at *Odes* 3. 1. 40, *post equitem sedet atra Cura*.

At line 25 the third section of the ode begins with a series of familiar propositions which would be wholly in accord with Epicurean thinking, although they are not quoted in any of the surviving writings of Epicurus. The notion that nothing is perfect is illustrated by the instances of Achilles, who won glory but had an early death, and Tithonus, who married Eos, the goddess of the dawn, and was given eternal life but not eternal youth. When old age came to him, she kept away from his bed but gave him food and ambrosia and clothing. When he could no longer move, she put him in a room and closed the door, and he lies there babbling endlessly and all his former strength is gone (*Homeric Hymn to Aphrodite* 233–8).

After these mythological exempla, Horace, not without some humour, contrasts himself with Grosphus. 'Around you a *hundred* flocks [*greges* would normally be sheep] and Sicilian cows are lowing', and while we may still be wondering whether cows are in flocks or sheep are mooing, a mare, fit to draw a *four*-horse chariot, adds to the noise by her neighing. Then, after the *four*-horse chariot, Grosphus wears wool *twice* dyed in the purple extracted from the shellfish *murex*, and we see the Horatian play with numbers which occurs also at the end of 2. 13 and 2. 19. In this stanza the repeated second-person pronoun, *te . . . tibi . . . te*, is a feature of the hymnic style (see on 2. 8. 21–4) amusingly misapplied in this context, as the stanza on Grosphus' opulence is the first in this ode which spreads into the stanza that follows.

Against this swollen splendour Horace sets his own blessings, not a hundred head of sheep and/or cattle, not pedigree race-horses, but his little bit of land on his Sabine estate. Small, too, delicate, fine, in the

---

XVII

Cur me querelis exanimas tuis?
nec dis amicum est nec mihi te prius
   obire, Maecenas, mearum
      grande decus columenque rerum.

a! te meae si partem animae rapit
maturior vis, quid moror altera,
   nec carus aeque nec superstes
      integer? ille dies utramque

ducet ruinam. non ego perfidum
dixi sacramentum: ibimus, ibimus,
   utcumque praecedes, supremum
      carpere iter comites parati.

Hellenistic style (1. 31, 2. 12. 1, and 2. 20. 1) is the breath of a Greek Camena. Horace often claims to have brought Greek poetry to Rome (1. 32. 3–4, 3. 4. 9–24, and 3. 30. 13–14) but never in bolder terms than these. Camena is the Latin Muse. To call her Greek says it in two words. In Plato divine inspiration is the presence of the god in the soul of the worshipper (see 2. 19. 6, 3. 4. 20, and 3. 25. 3). For us the spirit of the Muse is a bland metaphor; for Horace the Muse is breathing inside his breast. Further, Grosphus has his Sicily and Africa, but Horace has been able to combine Greece and the native Muse of Italy. And the power that gives all this to Horace is a Fate, whose name, *Parca*, connected with *parcere*, to spare, suggests that she is not Grosphan or overgenerous, but completely in accord with the simple life, which is an important theme of this poem. Even her adjective, *non mendax*, not lying, hints that the opulence of Grosphus is not entirely to be trusted. The ode is ending with the sound Epicurean doctrine that the benefits of the simple life, unlike fame, power, and wealth, are not at the mercy of public opinion, and so it looks back to the opening of this poem and forward to the themes of the first ode in the third book.

XVII

Why do you frighten me to death with your moaning?
It's no wish of the gods or of myself that you should die
    before me, Maecenas, my crowning glory
        and roof-tree of my house.

Come! If some blow strikes you first and carries off
the half of my life, what is there to keep
    the other half here? I like it less,
        the damaged half. That day

will bring ruin to both of us. I have taken my oath
and will not be false to it. We shall go, yes,
    we shall go whenever you take the lead, comrades
        ready to take the last road together.

me nec Chimaerae spiritus igneae
nec, si resurgat, centimanus Gyges
  divellet umquam: sic potenti
    Iustitiae placitumque Parcis.

seu Libra seu me Scorpios aspicit
formidulosus, pars violentior
  natalis horae, seu tyrannus
    Hesperiae Capricornus undae,

utrumque nostrum incredibili modo
consentit astrum: te Iovis impio
  tutela Saturno refulgens
    eripuit volucrisque Fati

tardavit alas, cum populus frequens
laetum theatris ter crepuit sonum:
  me truncus illapsus cerebro
    sustulerat, nisi Faunus ictum

dextra levasset, Mercurialium
custos virorum. reddere victimas
  aedemque votivam memento:
    nos humilem feriemus agnam.

Commentators suggest that Maecenas is a morbid hypochondriac, that Horace is exasperated by his moanings, and that in the fifth stanza of this poem he makes fun of Maecenas' belief in astrology by pretending that he has not even troubled to have his own horoscope cast.

None of this can be right. These are two men of immense intelligence and sophistication. Maecenas has made it possible for Horace to fulfil himself as a poet, and has made him rich. They have enjoyed each other's company for some fifteen years, and from the beginning in *Epodes* 1 and 3 Horace has addressed his friend and patron in intimate, affectionate, and humorous terms. There is no evidence for any cooling of their relationship and no chance that Horace is here brusque or impatient or peremptory, to choose but three of the commentators' adjectives. The whole of this ode shows rather the warmth of Horace's love for Maecenas, and the subtlety and cheerfulness of their conversation. This note will try to argue these points in order, first by considering the character of Maecenas, then by looking at the astrological problems, and finally by attempting to assess more closely Horace's tone of voice in the poem.

Odes 2.17

Not the fiery breath of the Chimaera,
not hundred-handed Gyges if he rose again,
will ever tear me from your side. Such is the decree
of mighty Justice and the Fates.

Whether Libra turns its aspect on me
or terrifying Scorpio, the more violent part
of my horoscope, or Capricorn,
the tyrant of the western wave,

our two stars are in wondrous harmony:
your protector Jupiter blazed back
at impious Saturn and rescued you,
slowing the swift wings

of Fate when the people in the crowded theatre
three times gave their glad applause;
as for me, the tree would have fallen on my head
and carried me off if Faunus,

the guardian of Mercury's men, had not parried
the blow with his right hand. Do not omit
to offer sacrifices and build a votive temple;
we will kill a little lamb.

We have seen on *Odes* 2. 12 that Maecenas was a man of affairs, sound in judgement and strong in action, sensitive and humorous, learned and sophisticated, loyal and affectionate. What then is the case against him? The only suggestion of hypochondria apart from this ode is the information in Pliny's *Natural History* 7. 172 that he suffered from continuous fever, *perpetua febris*, and had no sleep for the last three years of his life, 11–8 BC. But *perpetua* means that his insomnia was continuous, not that it was lifelong. There is no evidence at all for hypochondria, certainly not for hypochondria in 23 BC when this ode was published. Nor is the charge supported by the fragment of Maecenas' poetry cited by Seneca in one of his letters:

debilem facito manu,
debilem pede coxo,
tuber adstrue gibberum,
lubricos quate dentes,
vita dum superest, benest;
hanc mihi, vel acuta
si sedeam cruce, sustine.
(Seneca, *Epistles* 101. 11)

Odes 2.17

Maim my hand and
lame my foot,
stick a great hump upon my back,
rot my teeth and make them slack,
but one thing give—just let me live.
Give me that and I don't give a toss
if you make me sit on the prong of a cross.

This is obviously burlesque. Note the coarse Priapic metre, the jingling repetition of *debilem*, the assonance of *tub-* and *lub-*, the pleonasm of *tuber* and *gibberum*, the internal echo of *superest* and *est*, and the crashing climax of the opening dactyl in the last line instead of a trochee at *si sede-*, a feature which Aeschylus derides in his assault upon Euripides at Aristophanes, *Frogs* 1322. Only a philosopher could take this seriously. Maecenas had Epicurean leanings and the Epicureans jeered at those who hung on to life when it had ceased to give pleasure, as satirized and impersonated by Lucretius at the end of his third book, and here, surely, by Maecenas. There is no evidence of hypochondria. If he was a hypochondriac, that must be deduced from this ode, and this ode does nothing to support the idea.

Maecenas' moral failings, as listed by the philosopher Seneca in *Epistles* 114, and discussed above on 2. 12, include self-indulgence, self-display, and the lack of any desire to conceal his vices. Even when he was in charge of the city and on official business his dress would be casual and he would go through the streets escorted by two eunuchs. He also doted upon his wife. This testimony of Seneca is suspect, because he has a case to argue, namely that a corrupt use of language goes along with a corruption of character—*le style c'est l'homme*, or, as he himself writes in *Epistles* 114. 1, translating a Greek proverb, *talis hominibus fuit oratio qualis vita*. All the character failings of Maecenas, according to Seneca, are demonstrated by his style in writing and in speech, but Seneca's reading of the fragments of Maecenas' writings that he preserves does not give us confidence in his assessments. It would be wrong to condemn a writer of *dialogi* by selective quotation when we do not know the context, or even whether he is writing in his own voice, mocking the style of others, or putting words on the lips of a character. Besides, the Stoic philosopher is temperamentally out of sympathy with the hedonist, and Seneca may well have been inclined to take a jaundiced view of Maecenas because of the fact that Maecenas had been conspicuously more successful as a counsellor of Augustus than Seneca was as a counsellor of Nero.

Odes 2.17

The astrology of lines 17–22 is crucial to the understanding of this poem. 'Whichever of three signs of the zodiac *aspects* me', says Horace, 'our two stars are in wondrous harmony.' Scholars suggest that Maecenas was interested in astrology and cite a passage in the great Maecenas ode in Book 3:

iam clarus occultum Andromedae pater
ostendit ignem, iam Procyon furit
  et stella vesani Leonis,
    sole dies referente siccos.

(*Odes* 3. 29. 17–20)

The bright father of Andromeda
is already showing his hidden fire. Procyon
  and rabid Leo's star are already raging
    as the sun brings back the days of drought.

Here the father of Andromeda is the constellation Cepheus; Procyon is Canis Minor, the Dog who comes before (Greek *prokuon*) Canis Maior to announce the arrival of the Dog-days in August. This is astronomy rather than astrology, but it still may be true that Maecenas was interested in astrology. The very fact that it bulks so large in this ode suggests so, since Horace tends to tool his poems to their recipients. But even if that were the truth, it is not likely that Horace would be so inept as to mock the beliefs of a friend who thought he was dying. There is another interpretation which arises naturally from the astrological teaching current in the day, and which makes a poem that accords much better with the picture Horace elsewhere gives us of his relationship with Maecenas.

In modern journalistic astrology the horoscope is given by the sign of the zodiac with which the sun appears to go round the earth for the whole of the month in which the birth takes place. In ancient astrology, however, the ascendant and the moon sign were of greater importance. The ascendant is the sign of the zodiac which is rising above the horizon at the moment of birth. The moon sign, the crucial factor in Manilius' account of the zodiac in 4. 122–291 according to Housman's commentary (see Goold, p. lxxxv), is the sign of the zodiac in which the moon resides at the moment of birth. Given these technicalities it would be easy to explain this stanza in terms which admit of no sarcasm by Horace. He could well have been born when the moon was in Capricorn, and at a time of the day or night when Libra was just clearing the horizon and the next sign, Scorpio, was just about to rise. His ascendant would then have been in the cusp between Libra and Scorpio. Alternatively, if we accept the calculations of Nicklin based on Horace's birth-date of 8 December 65 BC, we could observe that the ascendant was indeed Libra/Scorpio. From there the fourth house provides the Lord of the Horoscope; on 8 December 65 BC that was Mercury, and on that date Capricorn was in Mercury. These are difficult questions and I am not competent to solve them. But even this superficial account makes it clear that lines 17–20 make sense astrologically. Horace knows that different signs are involved in his horoscope and we can once and for all reject the standard view that he is so blasé about astrology that he has not even bothered to find out his own horoscope. He is not ignorant and contemptuous, but aware of complexities.

What then are the two stars in line 21? The simplest explanation of this, against Nisbet and Hubbard (1978) and West (1991: 50), is that the punctuation at the end of the line is Fowler's colon, separating the invoice from the goods (see H. W. Fowler, 589, under 'Stops'). Our two planets (for *astrum*, 'planet' see *Oxford Latin Dictionary* s.v. 2) are in conjunction: Jupiter has saved you; Mercury, acting through his son Faunus, saved me. Horace is suggesting that Jupiter was the lord of Maecenas' horoscope, whereas his own lord was the much less important god/planet, Mercury. This interpretation is in accord with the exposition of these matters by Housman (908), who explains that signs of the zodiac 'do not rescue anybody from anything. A man's natal sign determines his character and pursuits, but for accidents and escapes from accidents he must thank the planets'. He goes on to explain, with citations from Greek astrological writings, that the principal beneficent planet is Jupiter and his principal opponent is the baneful planet Saturn. Many maladies are the gift of Saturn, and they can be mitigated by the intervention of Jupiter. On this analysis the rescue of Maecenas by Jupiter shining back, *refulgens*, at Saturn, is orthodox astrology.

When we move to Horace's rescue from the falling tree, which we have just taken with a pinch of salt in 2. 13, the tone lightens. Mercury, Hermes in Greek, is indeed a beneficent planet, but not powerful. Faunus, however, in line 28, has no part at all to play in ancient astrology. He was the Latin equivalent of the Greek Pan, son of Hermes. So Horace impishly suggests that the lord of his horoscope sent his Latin son to save his subject Horace, and a good reason for sending Faunus would have been that he was the god of the countryside and it would have been his duty to parry trees falling in Italy.

The lightness of touch towards the end of the poem is a typical Horatian turn, and even before this Horace has relieved the talk of death by a cheerful misuse of astrological terms, notably *aspicit* in line 17, where Horace considers which one of three signs is aspecting him. A sign of the zodiac does not have an aspect. The aspect is the angle at the observer between lines drawn from the observer to two heavenly bodies. It takes two to provide an aspect. As in the passage from *Odes* 3. 29 quoted above, Horace is anthropomorphizing celestial phenomena to reinforce what he wants to say at a human level. He will not desert Maecenas. The glare of a scorpion holds no terrors for him, 'although Scorpio creates spirits ardent for war and for the camps of Mars, and minds that take delight in copious bloodshed' (Manilius, 4. 220–1). Nor is he daunted by Capricorn although he is the ruler of the western seas (Propertius, 4. 1. 86) and prescribes for his children the calling of seafaring which is always close to death, *tenui discrimine mortis* (Manilius, 4. 570). Similarly, when a planet enters a sign of the zodiac, the two are in conjunction, but in line 21 Horace alludes to human emotions by saying that his planet agrees with, *consentit*, the planet of Maecenas.

This is typical Horatian humour in friendship, and miles away from the exasperation, impatience, and morbidity which commentators find in the ode. The *mise-en-scène* suggested is more like this. From the offerings mentioned in the last three lines of the poem we can deduce that Maecenas has been ill, and has recovered. From the first line we know that Maecenas himself is dubious about this recovery, and does not expect to live long. A hearty friend might respond: 'Nonsense! There's nothing wrong with you. You'll live longer than I will.' The first line of the poem almost says 'Nonsense' but Horace's line of argument is much gentler and more subtle. It may even be true that Maecenas had some credence for astrology, as did many intelligent contemporaries including Augustus, and had received a gloomy prognosis. Horace would then be rallying his friend to cheer him by re-interpreting the astrological data, coming to meet the sufferer on the sufferer's ground, an established tactic of all good counsellors, teachers, and friends.

What is the tone of the poem? Since this is Horace, it is elusive, and shifting, but the opening is unmistakable. 'Why do you make me half-dead with fright?' asks Horace and the verb *exanimas* is not a serious word. In *Satires* 1. 1. 76 the miser is asked if he likes lying awake all night *metu exanimem*, 'half-dead with fear' of burglars. In *Satires* 1. 4. 127 gluttons 'are petrified' (translations by Brown) when they see a funeral next door and the fear of death, *metu mortis*, makes them take more care of themselves. When the kitchen door opens in *Satires* 2. 6, the town mouse and the country mouse run round the kitchen in panic and, when the dogs start barking, they are out of their minds with fear, *exanimes trepidare*. In *Odes* 3. 12. 2 Horace is gently teasing young girls who fall in love and the lashings of their uncle's tongue, *exanimari metuentis*, 'scare them witless' (in a beautiful translation by Hodgson). In *Epistles* 2. 1. 178 the stage-struck playwright has the heart knocked out of him if he gets a dead audience, *exanimat lentus spectator*. Every time the word occurs in Horace, the tone is colloquial and the fear or distress of the sufferer is in some way absurd. So here, scholars who gravely expatiate on the sense of gloom which enters the poem in the first line are misunderstanding it.

The eight words which follow in the next line say it all. Having established the silliness of his own fears, Horace instantly leaves us in no doubt about his love for Maecenas, and the nine words in which he does so could not be simpler, *nec dis amicum est nec mihi te prius obire*, 'It's no wish of the gods nor of myself that you should die before me'. The stanza ends with a statement of what Maecenas has done for him. Far above Horace in wealth, power, connections, and breeding, he has given Horace his friendship and Horace is proud of it. He has also given him his protection, including the patronage which provided the living conditions which enabled him to work as a poet. Horace knew what he owed to Maecenas, and also knew how to express it.

In *Odes* 1. 3 he calls Virgil half of his soul or life, *animae dimidium meae*. Now Maecenas appears to be only an unspecified fraction, *meae partem animae*, part of my soul. On the other hand in Latin *duae partes* are two-thirds, *tres partes* three-quarters, *quattuor partes* four-fifths, and therefore it is easy to read *pars*, a part, as being a half (as in *Oxford Latin Dictionary*, 4b), particularly here, in view of what follows. This has been ravaged by emendation of the Latin text, but emendation spoils the simple arithmetic and the powerful sentiment. To provide a succinct translation, 'When part of my life is gone, why should I, the other part, delay, I, who would then not be so dear to me as the part which is gone, and that remaining part would not even be a whole, undamaged part?' Clearly the two parts in question are best thought of as halves.

In the third stanza, after Horace tells us that he has taken the military oath, he says: 'We shall go . . . we shall go, whenever you take the lead', as Maecenas did before Actium (*Epodes* 1. 1–6), 'prepared to take our last journey as comrades'—and they had most probably been comrades, *comites*, at Actium (*Epodes* 9. 1–10). If these epodes mean that they were on board ship together on this campaign, this is a powerful reactivation of their past. There is a bond between men who have faced death together.

After this high emotion, Horace lowers the temperature with some gentle mock-heroics. No power on earth could separate him from Maecenas, not the fire breathed by the Chimaera with its lion's head, its snake's tail, its Chimaera's body. This mythical beast is put to mock-heroic work also at *Odes* 1. 27. 24 as the equivalent of the fiercely possessive girl from whom not even the winged horse Pegasus could rescue the young man she had enchained. The Chimaera could not separate Horace and Maecenas, nor could they be torn apart even by the hundred hands of Gyges, who had joined in the assault on heaven and was now pinned in eternal torment under Vesuvius. This is the decree of Justice and the Fates, and the severity of this statement leads to the astrological argument already examined. Horace now gradually lapses into the colloquial and humorous as he describes the good offices of Mercury when the tree fell and would have carried him off. The verb *sustulerat*, literally 'had lifted', hints at the absurdity whereby a falling object could lift, an image we have already glimpsed at 2. 4. 11. The paradox is made more acute when the country god Faunus intervenes and expertly lightens (*levasset*) with his right hand the blow of the *falling* tree that would have *lifted* Horace.

We have come down a long way from the confrontation between Jupiter and Saturn which saved the life of Maecenas and now Maecenas is advised in mock solemnity not to omit to show his gratitude but to make sacrificial offerings and build a shrine to repay the gods for answering his prayers. By comparison Horace is small beer. He will make do just by killing a lamb, but even his modest ritual is touched by the mock solemnity of the royal we—'we shall kill a humble lamb'.

This is a poem of pure friendship, totally innocent of criticism or displeasure. Horace attempts to cheer his friend, he then praises and thanks him, and assures him that he is in no more danger of dying than he is himself. They will go together on their last campaign. Whatever Horace's horoscope indicates, the planets, who decide the time of death, have saved both of them. Maecenas is one of the great, and Horace of course knows his place, but as he reasserts his own humility, we can be sure that Maecenas smiled and knew that in friendship they were equals. The best comment on this poem is in Maecenas' will, opened when he died fifteen years after this ode appeared. In leaving his entire estate to Augustus he wrote 'Remember Flaccus as though he were myself.' Flaccus is Horace's intimate name for use by his friends.

The poem speaks not of a formal patron and client relationship, and not even of a comfortable middle-aged companionship, but of a deep sympathy, based on shared danger, shared pleasure, and shared sense of humour. Note the humour of *exanimas* in the first line, the reminder of wars survived in the third, the intensity of Horace's desire not to live if his friend is dead, and the sense of divine approval throughout, to which the astrological technicalities contribute. All this, and the repeated assertions and demonstrations of the ties between the two men, notably at *mihi te* in line 2, *te meae* (4), *utramque* (8), *utrumque* (21), and the balancing *te* and *me* in 22 and 27, repeated in the verbs in 31 and 32, suggest that these two men loved each other deeply. Horace says that he would not wish to survive his friend. When the time came he did so, but only by 57 days. Perhaps he was like Sir Albert Moreton's wife in Wotton's epitaph:

> He first deceas'd; she for a little tri'd
> To live without him; liked it not, and di'd.

XVIII

Non ebur neque aureum
mea renidet in domo lacunar,
non trabes Hymettiae
premunt columnas ultima recisas
Africa, neque Attali
ignotus heres regiam occupavi,
nec Laconicas mihi
trahunt honestae purpuras clientae:
at fides et ingeni
benigna vena est, pauperemque dives
me petit: nihil supra
deos lacesso nec potentem amicum
largiora flagito,
satis beatus unicis Sabinis.

Odes 2.18

There is a fragment of Maecenas' poetry, undated, which cannot be ignored in any assessment of this poem. The exuberance is Maecenatian (five Greek words in five lines) and the terms used in addressing Horace are normally the vocabulary of lovers:

lucente⟨s⟩, mea vita, nec smaragdos
beryllos neque, Flacce mi, nitentes
nec percandida margarita quaero
nec quos Thynica lima perpolivit
anellos nec Iaspios lapillos.

(fragment 2, Courtney)

I do not ask, my darling, for glowing emeralds,
nor, my dear Horace, for brilliant beryls,
nor dazzling white pearls,
nor lovely rings polished to perfection
by the Thynian file, nor stones of jasper.

XVIII

No ivory nor gold-coffered
ceiling gleams in my house,
no beams from Mount Hymettus
bear down on columns hewn in furthest Africa,
nor am I the unknown heir
of Attalus come to take over his palace,
nor do high-born women clients
trail their robes of Laconian purple for me,
but I have honesty, and a generous vein
of talent, and though I am poor, the rich man
seeks my company. I do not trouble
the gods for more or ask a powerful friend
for greater gifts, being blest enough
with the one and only Sabine country.

truditur dies die,
novaeque pergunt interire lunae:
tu secanda marmora
locas sub ipsum funus et sepulcri
immemor struis domos
marisque Bais obstrepentis urges
summovere litora,
parum locuples continente ripa.
quid quod usque proximos
revellis agri terminos et ultra
limites clientium
salis avarus? pellitur paternos
in sinu ferens deos
et uxor et vir sordidosque natos.
nulla certior tamen
rapacis Orci fine destinata
aula divitem manet
erum. quid ultra tendis? aequa tellus
pauperi recluditur
regumque pueris, nec satelles Orci
callidum Promethea
revinxit auro captus. hic superbum
Tantalum atque Tantali
genus coercet, hic levare functum
pauperem laboribus
vocatus atque non vocatus audit.

This is more like a sermon than an ode. More like an epode than an ode, it rattles along in a simple jingle (see Introduction, page xxi) and unlike the other odes it does not seem to fall into four-line stanzas. The three divisions printed above are purely to assist understanding. There is no ancient evidence for them. Odes are usually addressed to a person; they are often *poèmes d'occasion*, purporting to be responses to particular circumstances; they deal with love, friendship, conviviality, politics, the brevity of life; they are solemn, sublime, tender, teasing, burlesque, melancholy, cheerful, and often a combination of some such qualities. This poem, by contrast, is more nearly monochrome—lines 1–13, 'I am not rich but I have certain gifts'; lines 15–28, 'Why is the greedy rich man never satisfied?'; lines 29–40, 'Six feet of earth make us

Day treads on day,
new moons are hurrying to their death,
while you place contracts for cutting marble
the day before your funeral, building houses
with never a thought for your tomb,
struggling to push back the shore of the roaring sea
at Baiae's beach, and thinking yourself
a pauper because you are confined to land.
Yet all the time you are tearing up
your neighbours' boundary-stones and leaping
over your clients' walls
in your greed, while wife and husband
are driven out, carrying in their arms
their fathers' gods and their mourning children.

But no palace more surely
awaits the rich landowner
than the end rapacious Orcus
has destined for him. Why struggle to go further?
The impartial earth
opens for pauper and prince,
and gold could not suborn
the steward of Orcus to unbind ingenious Prometheus.
He confines proud Tantalus
and the lineage of Tantalus; he relieves
the poor man when his toil is over,
and whether called or not, he hears.

all of one size'. It sounds like the diatribe of a Cynic philosopher. And yet this is Horace, and it is poetry.

The first section (as the poem is divided in this text) contrasts the imported luxuries of the rich with Horace's own native treasures. The beams in the houses of the rich are of grey-blue marble from Mount Hymettus near Athens, and, with a colour contrast characteristic of Roman poetry, they bear down on yellow columns of *giallo antico* hewn in the quarries of Numidia in the north-west of modern Tunisia. To call that 'remotest Africa' is sound rhetoric, if not geography. When Horace says that he is not an unknown heir who has arrived to take over the palace of Attalus, he refers to Attalus III, king of Pergamum in Asia Minor, who in 133 BC bequeathed his whole empire, his capital, and his stupendous wealth to the Roman people in the forlorn hope of preserving it. Horace is not making an adverse comment on Roman imperialism, but merely making it clear that he is no *nouveau riche*. Nor do high-born ladies visit his house trailing gowns dyed with purple imported from Gythium, the port of Sparta on the Gulf of Laconia on the south coast of the Peloponnese, Laconia being the source of the best purple dye produced in Europe (Pliny, *Natural History* 9. 127). Wealthy Romans began the day by receiving complimentary calls from their clients, sometimes with their wives—Juvenal in *Satires* 1. 122 even shows us a husband dragging his sick and pregnant wife along for the morning *salutatio* in order to claim her daily dole, the *sportula*.

Wealth has been described in a coruscation of high-sounding foreign names, with Athens and Sparta framing Africa and Asia. Horace's only place-name refers to his modest estate in the Sabine hills, and he ends the first section with it. His wealth is not in showy architecture and imported luxuries, but in a list of qualities, all of which are cardinal virtues in a client with respect to a patron, expressed in terms which suggest that they are the equal of material wealth. *Fides* normally means trust, but can refer also to loyalty, discretion, reliability, the qualities which earn trust, and in this context it exploits as an overtone the fifth meaning in the *Oxford Latin Dictionary*, 'financial credit'. 'Talent' is the translation offered for *ingenium* but the word is used with a sense of its derivation, 'that which is inborn', thus powerfully countering all the exotica of the rich. His talent is lavish, *benigna*, 'open-handed, generous, liberal' (so *Oxford Latin Dictionary*, under *benignus* 2). The adjective hints that he too, like a patron, has riches to bestow. And there is a vein of them, as a mine has veins of the rich man's gold we met in the first line of the poem. This wealth of Horace is such that he does not have to cadge invitations nor pester the gods with his prayers nor beg a patron for more generous gifts. He has the Sabine estate which he owes to the generosity of Maecenas, and that is enough for him. He is sufficiently rich and blest (*beatus* here means both) with this estate, *unicis* suggesting that he is satisfied with this one thing, that it is uniquely wonderful, perhaps also that it is the only villa he possesses at this time. In half a dozen lines he has expressed his loyalty to Maecenas, his understanding of the relationship between them, his consciousness of the worth of his own poetic talent, his self-sufficiency, and his gratitude.

So much for the comparison between the rich man and Horace. Now at line 17 Horace moves to a denunciation of the rich man's rapacity. 'You are placing contracts the day before your funeral', where 'You' is the generalizing 'you', as often heard for example in the diatribes of the Stoic philosopher Epictetus and at the opening of Horace, *Odes* 3. 24. Congregations take an interest when the preacher is denouncing a fellow-worshipper in the next pew. The wealthy man is hectically busy: placing contracts for cutting marble, not thinking that the next marble that may be needed could be for his own sepulchre; building houses, not thinking that his next house may be his tomb; building out over the sea in an attempt to push it back, despite its *fortissimo* howls of protest; tearing up land markers (an offence in many cultures—'Cursed be he that removeth his neighbour's landmark. And all the people shall say, Amen', Deuteronomy 27: 17); dispossessing his own dependants, as forbidden in the *Twelve Tables* 8. 21 ('If a patron cheats his client, let him be accursed', *patronus si clienti fraudem fecerit, sacer esto*). As husband and wife are driven out of their home, they carry their household gods and their children, faces and clothes blackened to appeal for mercy as was the practice in the Roman courts (see on *Odes* 2. 9. 1). This sentence is an example of the dramatic effects made possible by the freedom of Latin word order, in line 26 the expulsion, in 27 gods clasped to the breast, in 28 the carriers (wife and husband in the nominative case) and finally the children they are carrying. This makes a mime of suffering piety, and might well shock Romans by reminding them of the similar scene at the beginning of their history, when pious Aeneas, the founder of Rome, had carried his father and his gods out of the burning city of Troy.

The link at lines 15–16 between the first and second sections, between the comparison and the denunciation, is one which no normal writer would have provided, 'Day is pushed out by day, and new moons come and rush along to die'. Unexpected as this is, it knits together the argument of the poem. So far the rich man has had a strenuous life, pressing and cutting in line 4, then, after seizing and dragging in lines 6 and 8, in line 17 cutting again, then building, struggling, shifting back, tearing up, leaping over, and driving out. Meanwhile, in the middle of all this, day is pushed out by day and new moons arrive and rush along in their haste to die. The days and the moons are as hectic as the plutocrat, and for them, as for him, the end is death. The rest of the poem is about death.

This third section has its own particular link with the second. The arrival of death has already been predicted in the building operations of lines 17–19 of the Latin—the rich man is frantically busy building great houses just before his funeral. Now the third movement repeats the theme in crashing chords—'No mansion . . . more certain . . . than the end predestined.' The end of the poem is full of mythology and the divine. Mercury was not bribed to free Prometheus, for all his cleverness (in Greek, *Prometheus* suggests fore-wisdom), nor did he free Tantalus and his royal descendants, including Pelops, Atreus and his son Agamemnon, Thyestes and his son Aegisthus, all of whom met notable deaths in Greek tragedy. After the still finality of death, which terminates all ambition and display, the poem ends with a coda which offers no escape to the rich, and wry comfort to the poor.

According to this analysis the odes consists of three clearly defined blocks of sense, but other readers divide it differently, and they are not wrong. Though we commentators find it helpful to talk in sections, this is not how Horace wrote. But however the ode is divided, its argument is knit together by means of responsions from passage to passage. Most clearly, all the three sections heard above are about houses, as for example in lines 2, 6, 14, 18, 19, and 31 of the Latin, and about boundaries and limits as at 11, 14, 21–5, 32, and 38. But there are more subtle cross-references. The gold of the first line is trumped by the lavish vein of Horace's talent. Nor did gold corrupt the steward of Orcus in line 36. Prestigious and exotic place-names are trumped by Horace's native talent and the thrifty Sabine country. Horace has no high-born lady clients, but in line 9 he asserts his own reliability as a client, and in line 25 sees clients traduced by the greed of the bad patron. The swift passage of time and the senseless haste of moons rushing to die are reminders to the rich man that he too will die, made explicit in lines 18–19, and hammered home at the end of the poem. The rich man is *avarus* in line 26, but Orcus is a match for him in rapacity in line 30. The children of the poor are maltreated but pauper and prince receive even-handed treatment in 33–4. Epithets, images, details, are not a random swirl but are interlocked and organic to the thought.

One word in the poem raises a serious problem. Who is *tu*, 'you' in line 17? It is normally taken, as above, to be a generalizing second person, 'You, any rich man'. On the other hand, Nisbet and Hubbard see that the immediately preceding lines point unmistakably to Maecenas, and remind us of Maecenas' wealth, of his palace on the Esquiline with its famous tower from which Nero was to watch Rome burn. They suggest also, at lines 7–8, that the trailing robes of distinguished ladies may recall the fondness of Etruscan women for voluminous coloured robes, and may therefore be an allusion to the retinue of the Etruscan Maecenas. They do not believe that Horace is rebuking his patron, rather that Horace 'exploits the ambiguity of *tu* to shift from the real Maecenas to the conventional plutocrats of diatribe (perhaps with an element of affectionate mockery)'.

Even this subtle and cautious proposition is to be resisted, let alone Lyne's interpretation (1995: 126–31) that Horace is 'imputing serious immorality to Maecenas'. The argument from women's dress carries no weight. Wealthy Romans took their wives along to the daily levees of the great, and Roman matrons wore a long dress with a coloured hem, the *instita*. Hence the trailing purple of line 8. Horace certainly addresses Maecenas elsewhere in tones of affectionate mockery (see *Epodes* 3 and 14), but he is a master of tact and discretion, a professed expert in the arts of the dependant (see *Epistles* 1. 17 and 18), and it is enough to remember the warm affection of the previous ode to make it certain that any such imputation of innuendo would be completely inconceivable in this ode. Horace was rich (see Introduction), and Maecenas rich beyond the dreams of avarice, but it is no surprise if some wealthy men disapprove of how some others use their money. Maecenas is not in any sense whatever to be associated with the acquisitive, impious, ruthless, plutocrat of this poem. Even the grammar tells against the suggestion. Maecenas is present in the poem in the tribute he receives in lines 10–14, but allusively and in the third person. The attack on the plutocrat begins sharply with the change to the second person *tu* in line 17. Horace has moved from a warmly respectful personal style into the sermon, and *tu* is the generalizing second person beloved of the preacher. In the second half of this book, in *Odes* 12, 13, 17, 18, and 20, Horace keeps coming back to his friendship with Maecenas, which is such an important and valued part of his life.

Who is the attendant of Orcus? Most scholars take this to be Charon, who ferries the dead over the River Styx, and accordingly they read *revexit*, 'carried back' in line 36. Whoever he is, he also keeps Tantalus under constraint, *coercet*, and brings relieving death to the poor man when he is weary with his labours. But Nisbet and Hubbard point out that Charon stays with his ferry-boat, answers prayers only from the dead on the bank, and brings death to no one. Mercury, on the other hand, the messenger of the gods, herds, *coercet*, the pious shades at *Odes* 1. 10. 18, and is the escort of the dead, the *Psychopompos*, pleasing to the gods above and the gods below at *Odes* 1. 10. 19–20. The steward of Orcus is therefore Mercury, and in line 36 *revinxit* should be read with six ninth- and tenth-century manuscripts. He himself was not captured by gold, *auro captus*, and did not unbind, *revinxit*, Prometheus bound—a typically dense and allusive Horatianism.

This note started with the intention of finding the poetry in this diatribe. It is nowhere more startling than in the last four Latin words.

When the poor man is wearied with his labours, Mercury 'whether called or not called, hears'. This is absurd. Not even a god can hear if there is no call. Or can he? This is Horace the surrealist going beyond reason to poetry.

For another demonstration of the generous vein of Horace's talent it is enough to look back at Bacchylides, fragment 21:

> There are no bodies of oxen, no gold,
>   no purple tapestries,
> but a mind well-disposed,
>   a pleasant Muse, and sweet wine
> in Boeotian goblets.

XIX

BACCHUM in remotis carmina rupibus
vidi docentem—credite posteri—
  Nymphasque discentis et auris
    capripedum Satyrorum acutas.

Euhoe, recenti mens trepidat metu
plenoque Bacchi pectore turbidum
  laetatur: Euhoe, parce Liber,
    parce gravi metuende thyrso!

fas pervicaces est mihi Thyiadas
vinique fontem lactis et uberes
  cantare rivos atque truncis
    lapsa cavis iterare mella:

fas et beatae coniugis additum
stellis honorem tectaque Penthei
  disiecta non leni ruina
    Thracis et exitium Lycurgi.

tu flectis amnis, tu mare barbarum,
tu separatis uvidus in iugis
  nodo coerces viperino
    Bistonidum sine fraude crinis:

Horace, *Odes* 2. 18 is therefore a 'motto' poem, like *Odes* 1. 18, 1. 37, and 3. 12 in the sense that it starts with a translation of the first line of a Greek poem. Even the structure of its argument (14 + 14 + 12) is reminiscent of the structure of strophe + antistrophe + epode in some of the simpler odes of Pindar and Bacchylides. There is, however, some difference in poetic texture between Bacchylides and Horace. Take the fourth line of the Bacchylides with its two different adjectives for the Muse and the wine, each of them meaning 'sweet'.

XIX

I have seen Bacchus among the lonely crags,
teaching songs—believe me, generations yet unborn—
and Nymphs learning them, and the sharp ears
of goat-footed Satyrs.

Euhoe! My breast is full of Bacchus. My mind
thrills with the terror I have just seen, and wildly rejoices.
Euhoe! Spare me, Liber, spare me,
fearful with your irresistible thyrsus.

It is no sin for me to sing of your wilful Thyiades,
of your fountain of wine and rich rivers
of milk, and again and again of honey
dripping from hollow tree trunks.

It is no sin to sing of the honour accorded
to your blessed wife now added to the stars, the palace
of Pentheus pitilessly torn to shreds,
and the doom of Thracian Lycurgus.

You change the course of rivers, you curb the barbarian sea,
and drenched with wine on distant ridges
you bind the hair of Bistonian women
in knots of harmless vipers.

tu, cum parentis regna per arduum
cohors Gigantum scanderet impia,
Rhoetum retorsisti leonis
unguibus horribilique mala;

quamquam choreis aptior et iocis
ludoque dictus non sat idoneus
pugnae ferebaris: sed idem
pacis eras mediusque belli.

te vidit insons Cerberus aureo
cornu decorum leniter atterens
caudam et recedentis trilingui
ore pedes tetigitque crura.

Can Horace be serious? The first stanza is clearly burlesque. He claims that he has seen the god Bacchus teaching songs to Nymphs in a lonely, rocky place. 'Believe this, generations yet unborn' is a clear warning not to, and he reinforces the warning by saying that he saw also 'the sharp ears of goat-footed Satyrs'. Here, with the feet and ears, there is the characteristic play of opposites, but Horace is also having particular fun with ears. Their sharpness is not simply an unnecessary descriptive detail. These ears are sharp because they are pricked up to listen to the music lesson. When Satyrs are within reach of Nymphs a certain type of behaviour is expected, but 'the sharp ears of goat-footed Satyrs' make it clear that on this occasion the Satyrs are listening intently and behaving properly.

'Euhoe!' opens the second stanza, the crazed cry of the Bacchants, the Thyiades, who run in ecstasy over the snow-clad mountains of Thrace. The Greek word *thuein*, 'to be mad' is in the picture here, as at 1. 17. 23 and 3. 15. 10. Such transports are surprising. Horace is not a 'Euhoe' poet.

But one of his gifts is the mastery with which he changes key, sometimes with subtle modulations as at 2. 16. 12 or 2. 18. 15, sometimes in a flash, as here. When he goes on to say that his mind is confused as a result of his recent fright, he might still be in the burlesque mode, he could be all of a flutter, but we do know that it is a fearful thing to look upon the face of a god and that Bacchus is a fearful god. He is not only a god of wine but also a god of poetry, and when Horace says that his breast is full of Bacchus, this is a direct statement of the experience of poetic inspiration, as explained in Plato's *Ion* 533–4 (see *Odes* 2. 16. 38, 3. 4. 20,

Odes 2.19

When the impious army of Giants scaled
the heights of your father's kingdom,
  you hurled back Rhoetus
    with your fearful lion's jaws and claws.

They said you were fitter for dance
and jest and play, not wholly suited
  to battle, but you were the centre
    of peace and war alike.

Cerberus saw you in all your beauty with your golden horn
and did you no harm, but gently brushed his tail
  against you and licked your departing feet
    and legs with his three-tongued mouth.

and 3. 25. 1–2). The god is in him. It is the god that speaks and not Horace. The confusion of joy and fear in line 6 is commonly experienced in epiphanies or in the *mysterium tremendum* as described by Lucretius when the teachings of Epicurus enable him to see the peaceful home of the gods in the atoms showering through the infinite void:

> his ibi me rebus quaedam divina voluptas
> percipit atque horror quod sic natura tua vi
> tam manifesta patens ex omni parte retecta est.
>
> (Lucretius, 3. 28–30)
>
> At the sight of these things a divine pleasure,
> and horror too, took hold of me to see that through you
> nature was so clearly opened and revealed in every part.

Horace knows something about this because he has sensed the visitation of the divine when engaged in poetic composition. Having explained his *euhoe*, he now repeats it, and begs this fearful god to spare him and not strike him with his dread, miracle-working staff, the thyrsus. This stanza is not simply a literary exercise, as some scholars assume. It starts with burlesque and moves to a description of the awesome experience of the inexplicable, which can occur in the course of poetic composition.

Sceptics will point to the renewed burlesque in the number games and freakish anatomy of the last stanza. Semele, whom Jupiter had been visiting in disguise, was tricked by Jupiter's wife Juno into asking him to appear to her in his true form. He came as the lightning and destroyed her, but rescued the baby from her womb and stitched it into his thigh until it was ready to be born. In due course this baby grew into the god

Bacchus and descended into the Underworld to rescue his mother. As he was returning to the light, according to Horace, Cerberus, the guard-dog of the Underworld, fawned upon him, and what a guard dog! It rubbed its tail against Bacchus, as a cat might do, and licked the feet and legs of the god. Much of what it licked was, presumably, bare skin, and note that this is a dog with three heads, a blatant reduction since 2. 13. 34, but still a grotesque picture made more grotesque by Horace's phrasing whereby it licked with a three-tongued mouth.

If these comments are right, the first and last stanzas of this poem are irreverent, and the second stanza is a serious statement of the role of the divine in the composition of poetry. This is an extraordinary suggestion, but then Horace is an extraordinary poet. Besides, although such freedom is not the way of contemporary Christianity, laughter may not have been so difficult to accommodate in the polytheistic religion of the Greeks and Romans. Other cultures have found it easy to worship gods and be amused by them. From Horace's point of view there is a benefit. He well understood that there are times when it is tactful to laugh as you tell the truth (*ridentem dicere verum*, *Satires* 1. 1. 24). Here he is making large claims for his poetry, and he may have sensed that large claims are more acceptable when presented with a tinge of humour. This is what he has done in *Odes* 1. 1, 1. 6, and 3. 4. 9–20.

The run of sense in the first four stanzas is important. Horace informs the reader that he has just seen Bacchus. Immediately he turns to address the god and tells him the effect of that vision. The third and fourth stanzas each begins with the word *fas*, claiming insistently that he is acting in accordance with the will of the god in singing of his achievements and of his worshippers. Presumably he is making this point firmly to Bacchus because he is aware that it is dangerous to blurt out the secrets of gods (see *Odes* 1. 18. 12–13 and 3. 2. 25–9). His defence is that in granting the vision described in the first stanza Bacchus has given him permission to make the revelations—how a blow of the thyrsus makes wine and milk spring from the ground, and honey flow from hollow trees; how Bacchus changed the bridal crown of his beloved Ariadne into the constellation Corona Borealis; how he destroyed the palace of the voyeur Pentheus and inflicted a hideous death on Lycurgus, king of Thrace.

The poem now moves into the hymn mode, signalled by the catalogue of achievements of the god which fills the last four stanzas, and the repeated use of the second-person pronoun (at lines 17, 18, 21, and 29 of the Latin). Most often such hymns end with a prayer, as at 1. 32. 13–16, but here no prayer is necessary. Horace has explained that Bacchus has inspired him, and has claimed authority to sing of the god. We can easily supply the unspoken prayer that the song will be worthy, will find acceptance, and that the inspiration will continue to be his.

A surprising feature of this poem and of the other Bacchus ode at 3. 25 is that they barely mention Bacchus' function as god of wine. It is also striking that each poem refers to his military prowess. A possible explanation may be found in the treatment of Cybele in Augustan Rome and in Virgil's Augustan epic the *Aeneid*. Cybele was a Phrygian goddess and part of the Augustan myth of the descent of the Julian family from the Phrygian city of Troy. But her rites were unRoman. Her priests castrated themselves to serve her, and her image was carried round the streets with alms-begging, flower-strewing, sword-waving, wild music, singing, and dancing, as described by Lucretius at 2. 600–32. To accommodate her to the Augustan religious ethos these rites were toned down and made much more orderly. Cybele was ring-fenced in the Rome of Augustus (see Wiseman). Bacchus, too, being an Olympian god, was part of the Augustan religious programme. He appears in his normal and central role in Horace in poems of love and wine, and this was clearly acceptable because it was part of Augustan cultural policy, as Horace saw it, to naturalize Greek lyric poetry in Rome. But he goes to some lengths to depict other and more respectable aspects of the god. So 1. 18 stresses the benefits of temperate wine-drinking and warns against excess, and 2. 19 and 3. 25 celebrate the role of Bacchus as a god of poetry. Horace is steering a tricky course. This may perhaps shed some light on the surprising adjective in the demand he makes to the young men at the symposium at 1. 27. 3–4 to keep *modest* Bacchus away from bloody brawls:

verecundumque Bacchum
sanguineis prohibete rixis.

From line 17 this poem contains many hymnic features, but has no trace of a prayer. This may point to a revealing feature of Horace's religion. The Epicurean believed that gods do nothing for men, that they are not interested in human life, but live in calm and blissful enjoyment of their own perfection. Yet Epicureans prayed. For them petitionary prayer was superstition, and valid prayer was purely contemplative. Its working could be explained in material terms. Sight for the Epicurean was the reception of a continuous flow of minute atoms pouring from the object to the beholder. By contemplating the perfect form of the gods, he subjected his own body to the effect of this bombardment of atoms streaming from the bodies of the gods, and his own form was duly affected and made more like the perfection of the divine. Horace, therefore, as one who was influenced by Epicureanism, had no need to ask for anything when he prayed. *Odes* 1. 10 and 2. 19 are examples of pure Epicurean prayer, as explained by Lucretius in a passage where he has been describing the folly of fearing the gods:

> quae nisi respuis ex animo longeque remittis
> dis indigna putare alienaque pacis eorum,
> delibata deum per te tibi numina sancta
> saepe oberunt; non quo violari summa deum vis
> possit, ut ex ira poenas petere imbibat acris,
> sed quia tute tibi placida cum pace quietos
> constitues magnos irarum volvere fluctus,
> nec delubra deum placido cum pectore adibis,
> nec de corpore quae sancto simulacra feruntur
> in mentis hominum divinae nuntia formae,
> suscipere haec animi tranquilla pace valebis.
> inde videre licet qualis iam vita sequatur.
>
> (Lucretius, 6. 68–79)

XX

Non usitata nec tenui ferar
penna biformis per liquidum aethera
vates, neque in terris morabor
longius, invidiaque maior

urbis relinquam. non ego pauperum
sanguis parentum, non ego quem vocas,
dilecte Maecenas, obibo
nec Stygia cohibebor unda.

iam iam residunt cruribus asperae
pelles, et album mutor in alitem
superne, nascunturque leves
per digitos umerosque plumae.

iam Daedaleo notior Icaro
visam gementis litora Bosphori
Syrtisque Gaetulas canorus
ales Hyperboreosque campos.

Unless you spew this out of your mind and push well away from you
all thoughts unworthy of the gods and foreign to their peace of mind,
those holy powers which you have sipped will often damage you
through your own fault; not that their supreme power can be violated,
or that they may know anger, and thirst for cruel punishments,
but because you will decide that beings who live peacefully
in quiet serenity are rolling great waves of anger down upon you,
and you will not approach their shrines with your heart at peace,
or be able to receive in quiet calm the particles which stream
from their sacred bodies into the minds of men to show the form of the divine.
From this you may see what sort of life may follow.

The dithyramb is a Greek poem in ecstatic praise of Bacchus, and Horace has been writing a Latin poem in praise of Bacchus. In contemplating the god while in the exaltation of poetic composition, he has known fear and joy, ecstasy and danger, a delicious danger, *dulce periculum*, he experiences also at *Odes* 3. 25. 18. He does not need to ask for anything. Epicureans, worshippers of Bacchus, and poets would understand this.

XX

It is no ordinary flimsy wing which will bear me
half-bard, half-bird, through the liquid air,
  nor shall I longer remain on the earth,
    but, grown too large for envy, I shall leave

its cities. I, who am of the blood of poor parents,
I, who come at your command,
  my beloved Maecenas, shall not die,
    nor be confined by the Stygian wave.

Already, even now, rough skin is forming
on my legs, my upper part is changing
  into a white bird and smooth feathers
    are sprouting along my fingers and shoulders.

Soon more famous than Icarus, son of Daedalus,
I shall be a harmonious bird and visit the shores
  of the moaning Bosphorus, the Gaetulian Syrtes,
    and the Hyperborean plains.

me Colchus et qui dissimulat metum
Marsae cohortis Dacus et ultimi
noscent Geloni, me peritus
discet Hiber Rhodanique potor.

absint inani funere neniae
luctusque turpes et querimoniae;
compesce clamorem ac sepulcri
mitte supervacuos honores.

In *Odes* 2. 19 Horace has claimed that his poetry has been blessed by a god, but at the beginning and end of the poem has softened the claim and made it more acceptable by giving humorous pictures of the god in action. So here in 2. 20 he uses a similar blend of the serious and the flippant, but this time it is not the god he mocks, but himself. He is a bard with two forms, *biformis vates*, now a bard, soon a bird. The term *vates* is high praise—he is priest, prophet, and poet, and the skittish translation offered above aims to catch something of this mock pomposity. As a bird he will fly with an amusing poetic singular on a wing which is unusual and robust—it would have to be to carry his paunch (see Suetonius, *Life of Horace*, quoted on p. 84). And he touches the sublime by flying through the liquid aether, which we know from Lucretius, 5. 281 and 500, and which Virgil too was exploiting in a prophecy, at *Aeneid* 7. 65, where bees are flying through the liquid aether, *liquidum trans aethera vectae*. Horace will soar up from the cities of Italy and of the whole Roman world, as we shall see before the end of the ode. Not for this white bird the black waters of the River Styx (*Styx atra* at Virgil, *Georgics* 1. 243). He will become a swan, the bird of Apollo, god of poetry.

Horace is hovering on the edge of the boastful and the pompous, but now he wheels away. In a sudden dramatic moment, *iam iam*, the prediction of the first two stanzas becomes reality. The change is beginning before our eyes, as he looks down and sees the skin on his legs roughening (the word *pelles* refers to animal hides, not human skin). We are glad that he does not discuss his feet. At the same time his upper body is turning into a swan with feathers sprouting along his fingers and he sees swan's down forming on his shoulders—his new neck would give him a good view. The elevation of the style is boosted by the anaphora of *iam* at the beginning of each of these stanzas. At line 9 *iam iam* means 'now, even at this very moment', whereas at line 13 the tense changes and *iam* has to be translated as 'soon', 'Soon he will be going to see . . . '. The

The Colchian will know me, and the Dacian who pretends
not to fear a cohort of Marsians, the Geloni
at the ends of the earth, the cultured Iberian
and the Rhone-swigger will learn me by heart.

Let there be no dirges or squalid mourning
or lamentation at my corpseless funeral.
Check your cries of grief and do not trouble
with the empty honour of a tomb.

English translator cannot follow Horace's sleight of mind. Horace is well aware that he is taking a risk in claiming to be changed into a swan. He revered Pindar and Pindar was the swan of Dirce, the spring of his home city of Thebes (*Odes* 4. 2. 25), but that very poem opens with the assertion that anyone who strives to rival Pindar will drown in the sea, as did Icarus, son of Daedalus, when the wax melted on his wings. Aware of this danger, Horace therefore makes fun of his own pretensions. The physiological embarrassments of lines 9–12 are the same tactic as we have just seen at the beginning and the end of *Odes* 2. 19. There too, he is making a large claim, and there too, humour renders it acceptable.

In line 13 he is more famous than Icarus and even here the tone is slippery to catch, since *notior* usually suggests notoriety rather than good fame, and since Daedalus flew but his son Icarus, having like Horace acquired feathers, soared too high and fell. But now the swan will visit the limits of the known world, a triumphal boast which is tinged with absurdity because in other passages where Horace tours the limits of Augustan power, he speaks in praise of the achievements of Augustus (so at *Epodes* 1. 11–13, *Odes* 4. 29–36 and 4. 5. 25–8) as Augustus himself was to do in his *Res Gestae* 26–7. There is, of course, no mockery of Augustus here, but perhaps a slight self-mockery at the expense of the Augustan poet who now makes this review of Augustan conquests in the body of a swan. The Bosphorus in Greek is the ford of the ox, and when the ford of the ox is moaning, *gementis Bosphori*, we are invited to hear the roar of the sea and the mooing of the ox against the tuneful cry of the whooper swan high above it, *canorus ales* in line 16. This is no ordinary swan, and we are reminded of that when in the midst of its world tour it visits a place that no man can ever visit on foot or by ship, the garden of Apollo in the inconceivably distant north of the world, the Hyperborean Plains.

The word *peritus* in line 19 means 'skilled, having expert knowledge' and has been much emended, but Nisbet and Hubbard are right in their commentary (1978) to take it as contributing to the humour of the passage. As things are, suggests Horace, there is little interest in Latin poetry among the Colchians (on the eastern shore of the Black Sea at the eastern limits of the known world) or the Dacians (on the lower Danube) or the Geloni (a semi-legendary branch of the Scythians at the northern limits of the world). On the other hand Romanization is more firmly established in Gaul and Spain, or, to take a swan's eye view, among those who live on the Ebro and swig the waters of the Rhône. All this fits well with the scandalous fate Horace cheerfully predicts for his book in the last poem of *Epistles* 1. He sees it as a young slave and prophesies that he will suffer all manner of abuse when he goes out into the world (West 1967: 17–19). Depilated and up for sale, he will soon be dirty and infested with worms and pawed by everybody in Rome, and have to go into exile in Utica in North Africa, or be sent bound to Ilerda in Catalonia, both ancient cities created *municipia* under Augustus, where Latin would have been much more important than it was among the Colchians, Dacians, and Geloni at the ends of the world, *ultimi*. In Roman eyes Gauls and Spaniards would have been comparatively well educated, knowledgeable, *periti*.

In the last stanza Horace lets it be known that he does not want to be mourned, and he calls mourning squalid because of the practice whereby the bereaved would befoul hair and toga with black ashes as a token of grief (see on 2. 9. 1 and 18. 28). But even here the wordplay continues. 'Let lamentations be absent from the empty funeral' is a literal translation of line 21, and *inani*, empty, in that context must indicate primarily that lamentation is useless. But the literal force of the adjective impels the mind to another common sense of *funus*, the second classification in the *Oxford Latin Dictionary*, namely 'corpse'. Horace's corpse will be empty. The wit is repeated in the last words of the poem, where Horace tells Maecenas not to give him the *supervacuos* honours of the tomb. Such honours are totally empty, in the sense of useless. So will Horace's tomb be, literally. The swan has flown.

So much for the self-deprecating humour of the piece, but throughout Horace is making serious points, sometimes glancingly, about his poetry. He is an extraordinary poet and he knows it, saying it with tongue in cheek in the first line of this poem, but gravely and impressively at the beginning of the next poem in the collection, *carmina non prius audita . . . canto*, 'songs not heard before I sing', a claim made by Callimachus and repeated by his Roman followers. On the other hand, Callimachus and his followers boast that their poetry is delicate, finely spun, as Horace himself does at *Odes* 1. 6. 9, 2. 16. 14 and 37–8, and *Epistles* 2. 1. 225. Here however from the opening words, 'This is no ordinary, no flimsy wing' he contradicts this, perhaps to suggest that although he has achieved Callimachean originality, he has retained a Roman robustness. He is not one of your normal Alexandrian poets. The Callimachean allusion is confirmed by a reminiscence of the epitaph Callimachus wrote for himself. At *Epigrams* 21. 4 he says that he sings songs more powerful than jealousy, *kressona baskanies*, and Horace translates that into Latin as *invidia maior* at the end of the first stanza of this ode. This refers to his own conviction that he himself, like Callimachus, has suffered from envy because of his poetry. He will allude to this at *Epistles* 2. 1. 89, and *Odes* 4. 3. 16.

The second stanza follows seamlessly on the first, since Horace suffered from envy also because of his friendship with the great, particularly Maecenas, as discussed for instance in *Satires* 1. 6. He there claims to have come from humble stock, and at *Satires* 2. 7. 29–35 he puts in the mouth of his slave a diatribe exposing his weakness for dinner invitations and describing the panic in the household if an invitation arrives from Maecenas. Maecenas calls, Horace goes. In the satire his own slave accuses him of servility. At 2. 18. 10–11 he has expressed his independence. Here he is deferential. This is a subtle relationship. The word *dilecte* in line 7 is not lightly used in Latin, and as Horace here claims that he will not die, this address to his beloved Maecenas in the last poem of the book is an indirect acknowledgement that what he has received from his friend and patron has made it possible for him to achieve immortality.

Most scholars take a more serious view of this poem and they are difficult to refute. They would argue that many of the touches which I find humorous are genuinely elevated. The single wing, for instance, is a standard Latin poetic singular and the liquid aether gives genuine elevation to the tone. On this analysis the poem is a solemn assertion of the immortality of his achievement. My view, on the contrary, is that in this ode Horace, as in 1. 1 and 2. 19, is serious, but not solemn.

If the poem is read in this way it produces an eloquent gradation in the three poems which end the three books of this collection. In the first, after the pomp and circumstance of the great Cleopatra ode, 1. 37, comes a tiny poem which sets the scene for a simple symposium Horace will enjoy with his young slave. The Augustan poet is letting it be known that he is independent, and allowed to be. Here at 2. 20 he is looking to the future fame of his works, but he is also deflating his own boastfulness.

The collection ends at 3. 30, where he looks back on his achievement without any coyness or irony, *exegi monumentum aere perennius*, 'I have built a monument more lasting than bronze'. The progression of these three final poems seems to be thoroughly Horatian. The interpretation also fits well with the poems about poetry in this second book—the cheerfulness of 2. 13, the complex tones of the poem to Bacchus at 2. 19 sandwiching lofty claims between the surrealism of the opening and closing of the poem, and now this burlesque about his immortality, whose message is clear although its tone is flippant. Should there be any doubts, we might remember that this book is full of *ad hominem* poems and the man to whom this poem is addressed is Maecenas, sophisticated, brilliantly intelligent, irreverent, independent, with Epicurean sympathies. He would have known how to read the swan. He would also have enjoyed the last stanza, which by a different route arrives at the same sensible conclusion as a fragment of his own writings preserved by Seneca in his *Epistles* 92. 35, *nec tumulum curo: sepelit natura relictos*, 'I don't worry about my tomb; Nature buries abandoned corpses.'

List of Works Cited

Auricchio, F. L., 'Per la concezione filodemea dell'adulazione', *Cronache Ercolanesi*, 16 (1986), 79–91.

Austin, R. G., *Virgil: Aeneid VI* (Oxford, 1977).

Bowman, A. K., Champlin, E., and Lintott, A. (eds.), *Cambridge Ancient History*², x (Cambridge, 1996).

Brown, P. M., *Horace: Satires I* (Warminster, 1993).

Brunt, P. A., and Moore, J. M., *Res Gestae Divi Augusti* (Oxford, 1967).

Collinge, N. E., *The Structure of Horace's Odes* (London, 1961).

Commager, S., *The Odes of Horace* (New Haven, 1962).

Connor, P., *Horace's Lyric Poetry: The Force of Humour* (Berwick, Victoria, 1987).

Conte, G. B., *Latin Literature: A History* (Baltimore, 1994).

—— see *Oxford Classical Dictionary* under 'Imitatio'.

Copley, F. O., *Exclusus Amator: A Study in Latin Love Poetry* (Ann Arbor, 1956).

Courtney, E., *The Fragmentary Latin Poets* (Cambridge, 1993).

Crook, J. A., 'Political History 30 BC to AD 40', in Bowman, Champlin and Lintott (eds.), *Cambridge Ancient History*², x. 70–112.

Davis, G., *Polyhymnia: The Rhetoric of Horatian Lyric Discourse* (Berkeley, 1991).

—— 'The Person of Licymnia: A Revaluation of Horace, *Carm.* 2. 12', *Philologus*, 119 (1975), 70–83.

Edwards, P. (ed.), *Thomas Kyd: The Spanish Tragedy* (Cambridge, 1959).

Ernout, A., *Pétrone: le Satiricon* (Paris, 1967).

Fiell, C. and P., *Modern Chairs* (Cologne, 1993), 46.

Fitzgerald, R., *Virgil: The Aeneid* (New York, 1983).

Fowler, D. P., and P. G., see *Oxford Classical Dictionary* under 'Literary Theory'.

Fowler, H. W., *A Dictionary of Modern English Usage*, revised E. Gowers (Oxford, 1965), 589.

Fraenkel, E., *Horace* (Oxford, 1957).

Gigante, M., 'Il ritorno di Virgilio a Ercolano', *Studi italiani di filologia classica*, 7 (1989), 3–6.

Goold, G. P., *Manilius: Astronomica* (Cambridge, Mass., 1977).

Griffin, J., 'Lyrical Moralising', review of Nisbet and Hubbard (1978) in *Journal of Roman Studies*, 70 (1980), 182–5.

Harrison, S. J., *Homage to Horace* (Oxford, 1995).

Hodgson, M., 'Neobule am Spinnrad', *Classical Association News*, 15 (1996), 15.

Horsfall, N., *La villa sabine di Orazio: Il galateo della gratitudine* (Venosa, 1993).

Housman, A. E., 'Ovid *Ibis* 512 and *Tristia* 3. 6. 8', *Classical Quarterly*, 9 (1915), 31–8, and in *The Classical Papers of A. E. Housman*, ed. J. Diggle and F. R. D. Goodyear (Cambridge, 1972), 905–12.

How, W. W. and Wells, J., *A Commentary on Herodotus* (Oxford, 1912), i. 292.

Kiessling, A., *Q. Horatius Flaccus Oden und Epoden* (Leipzig, 1890), revised by Heinze[10] (1960).

Klingner, F., '*Horazerklärungen*', *Philologus*, 90 (1935), 277–93.

Knauer, G. N., *Die Aeneis und Homer* (Göttingen, 1964).

Lebek, W. D., '*Horaz und die Philosophie: Die Oden*', in H. Temporini and W. Haase (eds.), *Aufstieg und Niedergang der Römischen Welt*, 2. 31. 3 (Berlin, 1981), 2031–92.

Le Corbusier, C. E. J., *Vers une architecture* (Paris, 1923).

Lyne, R. O. A. M., *The Latin Love Poets* (Oxford, 1980).

—— *Horace behind the Public Poetry* (Oxford, 1995).

Martindale, C., and Hopkins, D., *Horace Made New* (Cambridge, 1993), 5.

Mayer, R., *Horace: Epistles I* (Cambridge, 1994).

McKeown, J. C., *Ovid: Amores*, ii (Liverpool, 1987).

Michie, J., *The Odes of Horace* (London, 1964).

Mitchell, A., *A Field Guide to the Trees of Britain and Northern Europe*[2] (London, 1978).

Moles, J. L., 'Politics, Philosophy, and Friendship in Horace *Odes* 2. 7', *Quaderni urbinati di cultura classica*, 55 (1987), 59–72.

Morris, R. B., and Williams, R. D., 'The Identity of Licinius', *Philological Quarterly*, 42 (1963), 145–50.

Most, G. W., see *Oxford Classical Dictionary*, under 'Imitatio'.

Munro, H. A. J., *Lucretius: De Rerum Natura* (Cambridge, 1864).

Nicklin, T., review of Garrod's *Manilius Book Two*, *Classical Review*, 13 (1899), 271–4.

Nilsson, N.-O., Metrische Stildifferenzen in den Satiren des Horaz (Uppsala, 1952).

Nisbet, R. G. M., and Hubbard, M., *Horace: Odes Book 1* (Oxford, 1970).

—— —— *Horace: Odes Book 2* (Oxford, 1978).

Norden, E., *Die Antike Kunstprosa*[5] (Darmstadt, 1958).

Oxford Classical Dictionary, ed. S. Hornblower and A. Spawforth (Oxford, 1997).

Oxford Latin Dictionary, ed. P. G. W. Glare (Oxford, 1982).

O'Hara, J. J. *True Names: Vergil and the Alexandrian Tradition of Etymologising* (Ann Arbor, 1996).

Paget, R. F., 'The Ancient Ports of Cumae', *Journal of Roman Studies*, 58 (1968), 152–69.

Pasquali, G., *Orazio lirico* (Florence, 1920; reprint ed. A. La Penna, 1964).

Pelling, C., *Life of Antony* (Cambridge, 1988).

Quinn, K., *Horace: The Odes* (Basingstoke, 1980).

Reitzenstein, R., 'Philologische Kleinigkeiten 5', *Hermes*, 57 (1922), 357–65.

Schmidt, E. A., 'Schema Horatianum', *Wiener Studien*, 103 (1990), 57–98.

Segal, C., 'Horace *Odes* 2.6: Poetic Landscape and Poetic Imagination', *Philologus*, 113 (1969), 235–53.

Shepherd, W. G., 'Horace: The Complete Odes and Epodes with the Centennial Hymn' (London, 1983).

Syndikus, H. P., *Die Lyrik des Horaz* (Darmstadt: i, 1972; ii, 1973).

Weinstock, S., *Divus Julius* (Oxford, 1971).

West, D., *Reading Horace* (Edinburgh, 1967).

—— 'Horace's Poetic Technique in the *Odes*', in C. D. N. Costa (ed.), *Horace* (London, 1973).

—— 'Lucretius' Methods of Argument (3. 417–614)', *Classical Quarterly*, 15 (1975), 94–116.

—— '*Cur me querelis* (Horace *Odes* 2. 17)', *American Journal of Philology*, 112 (1991), 45–52.

—— 'In the Wake of Aeneas', *Greece and Rome*, 41 (1994*a*), 57–61.

—— *The Imagery and Poetry of Lucretius* (Edinburgh, 1969, London, 1994*b*).

—— *Horace Odes I: Carpe Diem* (Oxford, 1995*a*).

—— 'Learned Chit-Chat', *Joint Association of Classical Teachers Review*, 17 (Spring, 1995*b*), 4.

—— 'Reading the Metre in Horace, *Odes* 3. 9', in Harrison (1995*c*), 100–7.

—— 'Boys at Play', *Ad Familiares*, 11 (1996*a*), 6–7.

West, D., 'Petronius and Horace', *Classical Association News*, 15 (1996*b*), 7.
—— *Horace: The Complete Odes and Epodes* (Oxford, 1997).
Wickham, E. C., *Quinti Horati Flacci Opera Omnia*³, i (Oxford, 1896).
Wilkinson, L. P., *Horace and his Lyric Poetry* (Cambridge, 1945).
Williams, G., *Tradition and Originality in Roman Poetry* (Oxford, 1968).
—— '*Libertino patre natus*: True or False?', in Harrison (1995), 296–313.
Wiseman, P. T., 'Cybele, Virgil, and Augustus', in A. J. Woodman and D. West (eds.), *Poetry and Politics in the Age of Augustus* (Cambridge, 1984), 117–28.
Woodman, A. J., '*Eheu Fugaces*', *Latomus*, 26 (1967), 377–99.
—— *Velleius Paterculus: The Caesarian and Augustan Narrative* (Cambridge, 1983).
Zanker, P., *The Power of Images in the Age of Augustus* (Ann Arbor, 1988).

Brief Notes on Authors

The references are to page numbers, given only where the authors' works are discussed.

ANACREON (b. *c.*570 BC): Greek lyric poet 34–5.
ANACREONTEA (sixty-two poems in the *Palatine Anthology* attributed to Anacreon, but written in the first five or six centuries AD).
ALCAEUS (7th–6th century BC): Greek lyric poet 92–3.
ALEXANDER OF APHRODISIAS (1st–2nd century AD): Commentator on Aristotle.
APPIAN (early 2nd century BC): Author of Roman history in Greek.
ARCHILOCHUS (7th century BC): Greek elegiac and iambic poet.
ARISTOPHANES (*c.*455–*c.*386 BC): Greek comic poet 122.
ARISTOTLE (384–322 BC): Greek philosopher.
ATHENAEUS (early 2nd century BC): Author of *Deipnosophistae*, 'The Learned Banqueters', a polymathic dialogue.
AUGUSTUS (63 BC–AD 14): His *Res Gestae* was the official record of his achievements preserved at Ancyra in a copy updated after his death.
BACCHYLIDES (b. *c.*518 BC): Greek choral lyric poet 137.
BION (*c.*335–*c.*245 BC): Greek popular philosopher.
CALLIMACHUS (*c.*305–240 BC): Greek poet and scholar at the Alexandrian Library of the Ptolemies 78–80, 146–7.
CASSIUS DIO (consul AD 205 and 229): Author of Roman history in Greek.
CATULLUS (84?–54? BC): Lyric poet 39, 42–3, 86, 115.
CICERO (106–43 BC): Author of speeches, letters, and philosophical dialogues.
CRINAGORAS (*c.*70 BC–*c.*AD 15): Author of epigrams preserved in the *Palatine Anthology* 15–17.
EPICTETUS (mid 1st–2nd century AD): Stoic philosopher.
EPICURUS (341–270 BC): Greek Philosopher.
EURIPIDES (*c.*485–*c.*406 BC): Greek tragedian.
GELLIUS (AD *c.*130–*c.*180): Author of *Noctes Atticae*, 'Attic Nights', learned essays on mainly literary questions.

Herodotus (*c.*490–*c.*420 BC): Greek historian.
Hesiod (7th century BC): Greek didactic and mythological poet.
Homer (before 700 BC): Greek epic poet.
Ibycus (6th century BC): Greek lyric poet.
Juvenal (mid 1st century AD–*c.*AD 130).
Kyd, Thomas, 70.
Lucretius (*c.*98–*c.*55 BC): Didactic poet of Epicureanism 31, 112–4, 117.
Macrobius (5th century AD): Author of *Saturnalia*, a dialogue mainly on Latin literary subjects.
Menander (394/3–342/1 BC): Greek comic poet.
Milton, John, 30, 101
Ovid (43 BC–AD 17): Poet.
Palatine Anthology: A collection of Greek epigrams written from the 4th century BC onwards, compiled around AD 980.
Panegyricus Messallae: A eulogy of M. Valerius Messalla Corvinus preserved as 3. 7 or 4. 1 in the Tibullan corpus.
Petronius (1st century AD): Author of the *Satiricon*, a satirical novel 45–6.
Philodemus (110–*c.*38 BC): Greek epigrammatist and philosopher.
Philostratus (4th century AD): Greek author of *Eikones*, descriptions of pictures.
Pindar (518–438 BC): Greek choral lyric poet 16, 114–5.
Plautus (before 251 BC–at least 184 BC): Latin comedian.
Pliny the Elder (AD 23/4–79): Encyclopaedist.
Pliny the Younger (*c.*AD 61–*c.*112).
Plutarch (before AD 50–after 120): Greek biographer and essayist.
Pope, Alexander, 62.
Propertius (*c.* 50 BC–after 16 BC): Writer of elegies produced 28–16 BC.
Quintilian (*c.*AD 35–before 100): Writer on rhetoric.
Sappho (7th–6th century BC): Greek lyric poet 37, 92.
Seneca (*c.*2 BC–AD 65): philosopher and tragedian.
Shakespeare, William, 91.
Simonides (*c.*556–468 BC): Greek lyric poet.
Suetonius (after AD 70?–after 122): Biographer.
Tacitus (*c.*AD 56–after 118): Historian.
Teles (3rd century BC): Cynic philosopher.
Tibullus (55?–19 BC): Writer of two books of elegies produced in 26–25.
Theocritus (early 3rd century BC): Greek pastoral poet.
Twelve Tables (traditionally 451–450 BC): The basis of Roman law.

VARRO (116–27 BC): Polymath.

VIRGIL (70–19 BC): Writer of *Eclogues* in 39 and *Georgics* in 29. The *Aeneid* was edited after his death in 19 BC.

Index of Topics

Figures in brackets refer to pages where the feature is discussed but not so named.